STUFF
THE
MUSIC
BUSINESS

THE DIY GUIDE TO MAKING IT

Printed by: MPG Books Limited, Bodmin, UK

Published by: Sanctuary Publishing Limited, Sanctuary House,
45-53 Sinclair Road, London W14 0NS, United Kingdom
Web site: www.sanctuarypublishing.com

ISBN: 1-86074-276-9

STUFF THE MUSIC BUSINESS

THE DIY GUIDE TO MAKING IT

Will Ashurst

acknowledgements

This book is dedicated to any musician or manager who opened their post one morning to find a letter from a record company beginning "Thank you for sending us your material", and to any who have sat in a battered Transit outside Watford Gap services at 4am wondering if they can afford a pot of tea. It's also dedicated to anyone who does not believe that the music business begins and ends with the record companies.

I would like to thank Jez for his help with the appendices and some of the other material in the book, and also say a belated thanks to erstwhile treeclimber Ollie Smith for help and hilarity over the years.

Thanks also go to the Tiny Bloke for the office, and special thanks as ever to Charlie Walker for supplying Stella Artois in times of stress.

contents

introduction **9**

chapter 1 motivation 19

chapter 2 setting up...29

chapter 3 recording...49

chapter 4 mastering, artwork and manufacturing 63

chapter 5 distribution 69

chapter 6 marketing and promotion 77

chapter 7 touring...87

chapter 8 the internet...101

chapter 9 merchandising..113

chapter 9 licensing 119

epilogue 133

appendix 1 sample licensing agreement 135

appendix 2 London rehearsal rooms......................................140

appendix 3 regional rehearsal rooms.....................................142

appendix 4 regional club venues...144

appendix 5 London club venues 147

appendix 6 artwork designers...150

appendix 7 manufacturers and duplicators 153

appendix 8 merchandising companies....................................156

appendix 9   web site designers 159

appendix 10   useful web sites...162

appendix 11   music industry accountants..165

appendix 12   music industry solicitors 168

appendix 13   music industry organisations 171

appendix 14   press and PR companies 174

appendix 15   music publications...177

appendix 16   distributors 181

introduction

At the tail end of 1999, I was driving through the West End of London, past some old haunts, when I turned into Manchester Square and was greeted by the sight of the old EMI building at Number 20 being demolished. I parked up and had a look. This was the building I'd arrived at on my first day in the music business, the building in which The Beatles had been photographed, leaning over the balcony, for the covers of the *Red* and *Blue* albums. It was also the building outside which Sigue Sigue Sputnik had been photographed when they signed their deal, but I'm still trying to blot that out.

I had no idea that they were knocking down 20 Manchester Square. EMI themselves had moved out years ago, to plush new offices in Hammersmith, but the building still had a real pull for me. Some say that everyone in the music business has worked for EMI at one time or another; it's the last British major record label, one of the oldest record companies in the world and an institution, in almost the same way as the BBC.

Seeing the heaps of grey concrete and tangled metal made me think just how much the music business had changed in the 15 years in which I've been attempting to make a living from it. In the mid 1980s the majors ruled the roost completely, with huge numbers of artists signed to them, enjoying ridiculously excessive marketing and A&R budgets. Independent labels of any significance were few and far between – some were hanging on grimly in the aftermath of the heyday of Punk and New Wave in the late Seventies, and other embryonic labels in the dance field were waiting in the wings for the Acid House boom of 1987 and 1988.

In a way, the demolition of the old EMI building was symbolic of the enormous changes that the music business is beginning to experience. A few weeks after the final traces of 20 Manchester Square were erased, EMI merged with Warner Music. At one fell swoop, the biggest music company in the world was created, which was controlled by an online company formed less than ten years previously. The fallout from the EMI/Warner deal will take a year or so to assess, but there are a few clear certainties, at least if the Seagram purchase of PolyGram is anything to go by. Firstly, more artists will be dropped by EMI/Warner than are signed – there will be a huge clearout of dead wood. Secondly, thousands of people will lose their jobs and the people who manage to keep them will have to work twice as hard.

The media speculation concerning the reasons behind the EMI/Warner deal rested heavily on the synergies provided by Time Warner's previous merger with AOL, as well as more humdrum motives such as cost-cutting in areas such as distribution and manufacturing. The theory seems to be that record companies must stake their claim in the online revolution in order to survive, and artists must adapt to a new arena, which may eventually see the death of the traditional album release.

So what are the factors that have led to such sweeping changes? In the new millennium, the majors' grip on the global music business may not be exactly under threat but, for the first time, they are looking vulnerable to the one group of people they had been used to controlling absolutely: the artists themselves. It's as though the global music business – which was once thought to be mysterious, all powerful, and beyond the challenges of mere mortals – has been revealed as a gigantic con trick of Wizard Of Oz proportions. The consequences of this new philosophy have spread throughout the business, from the reduction in the manufacturing costs of CDs and the advent of CD-R through to the explosion in music activity on the Internet.

Of all the changes that the industry is going through, its approach to the Internet is probably the most critical to its continued health. The furore of decades ago which greeted the arrival of home cassette technology (remember the skull and crossbones 'home taping is killing music' logo?) is nothing compared to the hysteria with which the industry has approached the MP3 revolution. Well, home taping didn't kill music, and neither will MP3. Although there is a real and significant danger of piracy eroding the record companies' and publishing companies' revenue streams to a small extent, the new opportunities presented by the Internet should easily outweigh the downsides. There has been a scramble amongst record companies to establish their own web sites and make their catalogue and new tracks available to be downloaded at a price. EMI has bought musicmaker.com, which offers the ability to create compilation CDs from some of EMI's huge warehouse of tracks, and Universal has launched its own site, farmclub.com, aimed at finding new artists and offering them a deal. Through the Internet, fans of bands across the world now have access to artists' official and unofficial sites and newsgroups, creating new interest in the established activities of artists. (These days, tour dates and release news appear on the Internet well before they appear in the press.)

In terms of retail, the Internet revolution has gathered pace quickest of all. Both independent online retailers (such as Yalplay and CdNow) and established high street retailers (such as HMV and Tower Records) are competing in a market which is estimated to be worth $4 billion by 2004. There is a huge debate amongst retailers about the future of traditional record retailing: should they continue to invest in high street stores, or should they concentrate on developing a strong online presence? To use the jargon, is it to be clicks or bricks?

Perhaps most significantly, however, for the first time there is a true and credible alternative for new and established artists to market their work, other than simply signing to a major record company.

When one begins to analyse this sea change in the operations of the music industry, odd questions begin to crop up. Who cares about the label on which a record is released? After all, people don't look at a movie poster and think: 'This is bound to be great – 20th Century Fox are distributing it!' They check to see who is starring in it, they look at the press quotes on the poster, and hopefully they remember a few snippets of the movie they may have seen on a TV movie review show. There is a long history of hugely successful independent films which have attracted the public because of the talents of the stars, the director and and the screenwriter, rather than the distributor. Why does the music business have to be any different?

Historically, the difference has always been money. Only a major label with enormous budgets (or an independent label with excellent global licensing deals) has ever stood a chance of breaking a band internationally on a large scale. The sheer cost of mounting an effective global (or even national) marketing strategy means that simply making more than a small amount of people aware of a new band is hugely expensive. Even after the advent of promotional videos in the mid 1970s – which were supposed to remove the need for artists to slog round the world, performing on TV shows – the philosophy of the majors is that huge marketing budgets are still the order of the day.

One could argue that, even though no one really cares who distributes or produces a movie, the mere fact that it *is* produced and distributed at all is purely because of financial investment. The fact that people know about the movie to talk about it at all, and recommend it to their friends, is down to the marketing budgets that paid for the poster to be put up in the first place. But this is a self-fulfilling prophecy. Because of the huge budgets which the major studios deal with in order to produce their movies in the first place, implementing massive marketing budgets is the only way of allowing the possibility that the movie might recoup and make money.

It's a little strange, then, to watch the movie studios quake at the growing influence of web sites acting as a global forum, in which real people can review movies; strange also to see them scrambling to get on the bandwagon of movies such as *The Blair Witch Project*, which owe a huge amount of their audiences to web-generated hype.

For decades, major record companies have been entrenched in the same way of thinking. Because of the huge numbers of people who work for them, and because of the sheer scale of their worldwide operations (not to mention the pressure from their shareholders), they are incapable of operating on anything other than a massive scale. Their distribution systems are complex and expensive, they have enormous offices, they pay large salaries, and they have huge numbers of artists on their rosters. This level of operation, coupled with the very low success rate enjoyed by the majors in relation to the number of bands they sign, can only work in one scenario: that in which they control the music business absolutely – in other words, they own all of the copyrights, most of the distribution, at least some of the stores, and (ideally) they exercise some level of control over the media. Their ideal scenario would be one in which they could perhaps operate an unofficial cartel, also controlling prices.

One of the most marked differences between the movie business and the record business is simply the cost of production; and this could explain why the new technologies and philosophies are more damaging to the major record companies than to film studios, for the fact is that you can make a great record for next to nothing. Whether you have your own studio equipment in your basement or bedroom, or whether you can cut a deal with a studio, the production costs could be negligible. Also, once you've made your great record, you can reproduce CDs of it for as little as 60 pence, or a dollar, even if you are manufacturing limited quantities. No movie maker can produce a feature film – including hiring a crew and actors, paying for post-production, the making of prints and distribution – for next to nothing. Not even close.

This doesn't alter the fact that, for decades, artists have thought that the only game in town was signing to a major label, as though no real alternative existed. Bands signed to a small independent labels in the UK were effectively at the mercy of the label's bank manager and its overseas arrangements, which would often be a patchwork of ineffective licensing deals with similar small labels. Inevitably, the more interesting indie labels were either bought out by the majors or taken under their wing by way of licensing and distribution deals. At worst, even if a band has only a limited amount of success on an independent label, they are at risk of not receiving payment, or the company itself collapsing if one or more key employees left. Often, the very factor that made an indie deal interesting was the maverick and often autocratic figure who ran the label, which often proved to be a double-edged sword if that person decided to change tack completely.

One of the more significant events in the UK music industry, on the cusp of the millennium, was Alan McGee's decision to quit Creation Records, the company he founded in the early 1980s. Unless readers have been living under a rock, Creation must be accepted as probably the coolest, most credible, exciting and yet (certainly from the time Oasis signed) financially successful and secure 'indie' label that has ever existed in the UK. McGee cited numerous reasons for quitting the label, but the underlying sentiment was that he wanted to be surfing the tsunami of change that is currently battering the UK industry, rather than be drowned by it. He estimated that, in the last few years, around 30% of bands signed to major labels have been dropped and around the same percentage of employees had been made redundant, and I can't see any reason to disagree with these estimates. Artist rosters have certainly been trimmed, and to a much larger extent than can be put down to simply removing the last of the Britpop stragglers and correcting the A&R failures of unsuccessful genres such as drum 'n' bass.

What we appear to be left with are major record labels which have two types of artist: one is the globally-successful, often ageing rock/pop star who releases albums every three or four years and maintains a successful live career whatever the sales of their current album; the other forms part of a quite phenomenal imbalance in the majors' rosters that has arisen globally since the late 1990s – the rise of pop. By 'pop', I mean the genre which specialises in manufactured and highly marketed artists who, in the main, neither write their own material nor have any hope of a career lasting more than a couple of years, and whose core audiences are primarily aged 14 and under. It's easy to understand why the majors have rushed towards pop: firstly, there is the need to create product to feed their global machine; and secondly, there is a theory that pure pop occasionally leads to the development of artists who can cross over to another genre and develop an adult mainstream audience (George Michael, for example).

It is still the case that, with a talented and marketable artist, majors can push the boat out on a global scale and carry on pushing it out until sales success is achieved. They play for high stakes, and the money they make from just a few successes is enough to carry the large number of unsuccessful projects they undertake. Due to the sheer amount of money a UK major will spend in order to achieve sales targets, there is almost no room for manoeuvre below platinum or multi-platinum sales, and preferably some significant sales success should be achieved outside the UK. Without wishing to generalise, any UK major who signs an act, releases a couple of singles with averagely expensive promo videos and carries out a reasonable amount of marketing will lose money if the act only sells 100,000 albums.

Let's just think about that for a second. 100,000 albums! What kind of sums of money are we talking about at sales levels like this? Well, you can assume that the record company gets about £8 per sale after offering discounts to shops from its printed wholesale price. From this they have to deduct payments to songwriters/publishers, totalling about 70 pence on each record. They then have to pay for manufacturing, distribution, recording, the band's own advance, the producer, tour support, making a couple of £30,000 videos, flying the band down to a Radio One roadshow, drinks with Chris Evans' producer – there's no way they can have made any money so far, particularly if you factor in the sheer cost of people's time. It doesn't matter which part of the company's investment is 'recoupable' against the artist's royalties at sales levels like this – the company has lost money.

Going back to the analogy of a movie, the one major factor that the movie business has always been able to exploit is word of mouth. Because the act of going to see a film is a night out, and an event in itself unlike the first hearing of a new album, people have always told their friends when they have seen a great (or terrible) new film. However, because musical taste is so diverse, it never works in quite the same way; people don't rave to their friends about new records unless the friend is a huge fan of the same band, or of the same genre of music. Instead, the most successful records tend to drift into the subconscious if they are experiencing heavy airplay on the radio, if the band is on television three times a day, and if the reviews are favourable.

One of the most important points made by McGee in summing up his decision to quit Creation related to the Internet. He pointed out that, in the future, bands such as Oasis would have no need of record companies. All they would need would be their fans' email addresses, and they could sell them their next album directly for around £10. Although this sounds right in theory, this brave new world assumes that all bands have such a huge hard core of fans eagerly awaiting their next release that it will be enough to simply let them know about it. In practice, the experience of recent years has shown us that the number of die-hard fans enjoyed by even a major band can in fact be relatively small. There has been a succession of albums by major artists which have underperformed enormously, compared with the sales levels of a previous release. This suggests that there are a large number of floating voters in every band's perceived fanbase, to whom the purchase of a new album is not necessarily a certainty.

If a superstar act in the UK is defined as one which sells over a million albums, then it's rare that any such act sells such an enormous amount of records without a series of hit singles, touring, and a high media profile. One of the best examples to cite is Robbie Williams: after leaving Take That, and after a year of almost never being out of the papers, one could have been forgiven for thinking that his debut album would have been guaranteed to go at least gold (100,000 sales). Even with a big first hit, with 'Freedom', it has passed into industry folklore that at this point his debut, album *Life Thru A Lens*, had only sold around 30,000 copies. It took the huge success of 'Angels' to kick-start things, launching the album, and Robbie's solo career, into the multi-platinum stratosphere.

There is one indisputable rationale that underpins McGee's thinking, however: if Oasis really did sell CDs directly to the customer for around £10, along with postage and packaging, then it would be astonishing if the band were not able to generate a £6 profit margin on such a sale. After all, at the levels of unit manufacturing they would require, the hard costs of producing the CD, inlay card and jewel case is unlikely to exceed 40 pence. It would be reasonable to assume a marketing cost of around £1.50 per unit. Even if a traditional distributor were employed to fulfil the orders, and allowing for credit card charges, a £6 margin would be about right. Yet I would doubt that even Oasis earn a record royalty greater than £1 per CD under their deal with Creation/Sony for a sale in the UK, never mind overseas.

So, £1 versus £6. One can look at this in two ways. If they sell the same amount of records that they always have then they would make seven times the amount of money. Alternatively, they only need to sell one sixth of the records they do now to make the same amount of money – perhaps by doing a lot less work. Additionally, it is simply a plain fact that a UK record company will pay less for a sale overseas than for a sale in the UK; but sell the CD yourself and you can earn about the same in every major territory around the world.

So where does all this leave us? Marketing and distribution. The bedrock of the global entertainment business, be it movies, computer games or records, is marketing. Assuming that the product is of suitable quality and the reviews are favourable, the potential global audience for an album is in the tens of millions, and the foundations are there to build an artist with a career sales total of possibly hundreds of millions of records. Sign to a major label, make a great record that all of their overseas companies love, and it's possible that you could be marketed to success and riches.

Secondly, there is distribution. No matter how great the product, and no matter how brilliant the reviews, if people can't buy it or experience it then it will fail. With major distribution muscle, however, record racks across the world will bulge with that album simultaneously, as part of a huge sales strategy.

But what if you can't get a deal with a major? What if, despite your best efforts, they just don't understand your music, or like it, or think that it fits in with this year's strategy? What's the alternative? The answer is that there are now two alternatives, where there used to be one. Being rejected by a major used to mean trawling around to find a deal with an indie label, perhaps just in the artist's home territory, and scraping together a few overseas deals.

This is still a viable first alternative. Every country which has a developed music industry will have a number of labels which qualify as credible and 'cool' amongst opinion-formers in that country, by which I mean those in the media. Some musical genres lend themselves more easily to developing a network of worldwide independent labels that are extremely credible and successful in their field; for example, the rock/metal genre has always had a tradition of solvent, successful and creative independent labels, bringing new and innovative artists to the public attention, some of which would inevitably land deals with major companies in due course. So if a band were in the position of owning their own album (perhaps after having been dropped by a major company), then it's certainly possible that licensing deals could be negotiated with a network of credible labels around the world, which would push the record in each one of those territories.

Although this sounds good in theory, the reality is that it will often be a matter of luck rather than judgement that such arrangements lead to significant sales in a particular territory. It's unlikely that the band will be able to deliver all of the required elements for significant sales to occur – for example, a promotional video, or a tour in that territory, or even a promotional visit – and after calculating how many additional sales are likely to result from the increased expenditure, the label may decide that it isn't cost-effective to pay for such expenses.

Another downside of trying to deal with a patchwork of licensing deals around the world is that it's almost inevitable that the label in the band's home territory will actually want to sign the band outright and conclude overseas deals itself, splitting the income with the band. In such a scenario, some of the perceived advantages of going the indie route – such as creative freedom, and not being tied to a long contract – can become eroded to the extent that what is left is more or less a major-type deal, but with much less money.

The second alternative is the newest and most exciting, and offers the most freedom. In theory , by controlling their own recordings, setting up an active website and linking in some key licensing deals, artists can have the best of both worlds. The ultimate goals under this scenario can be listed as follows:

• That creative control rests solely with the artists, in terms of the recordings they make

• That the artists own and control their own recordings, rather than allowing record companies to own the copyright in them

• That the artists have as much control as possible of the sale and distribution of their recordings, and sell at least a certain percentage of them directly to their audience

• That the artists derive the maximum possible income from the sale of their recordings

• That if deals need to be concluded with other parties in order to distribute the artist's recordings, such deals are one-off arrangements which do not tie in the artists to long contracts.

As the music industry begins to grapple with the new vista opening up before it, all bets are off. We can only begin to guess at the landscape of the industry in five or ten years' time. The only certainties are that the way in which people listen to music and purchase music will change dramatically, and perhaps even the way in which people perceive music as part of their lives will alter. But the most important certainty from the reader's perspective is that there will always be musicians making music that deserves to be heard. A brave new world for artists has certainly arrived. It's only a case of learning how to make it work to your advantage. Hopefully, this book will help.

motivation

You're reading this book because you want to make your own records and release them. What's your motivation for this? It could be that you've been punting your material at record companies for years and not getting anywhere, and the post has brought you a steady stream of rejection letters. You may feel that nobody in the traditional record industry understands your music, or appreciates your songs. You may think that the songs in the charts are rubbish in comparison with your own material, and you can't understand why they are hits. Every rejection fires you with righteous indignation at the short-sightedness of the world at large in not recognising your obvious talent. If you have had some dealings with the music business, it could be that you are extremely sceptical of the abilities of the people you have met, and feel that you could do a better job yourself.

These reasons are primarily negative, and are no basis on which to make a commitment to releasing your own records. They are a recipe for disappointment and possibly the loss of a fair amount of time and money. Who knows? It could be that your music just sucks, that you have little or no talent, and the only other person who thinks you are great is your mum! This may be harsh, but it's realistic.

On the other hand, you could be a gigging band with an enthusiastic crowd of supporters which is growing steadily. You could have a mailing list, and some supporters on the local paper. Maybe you've started to get some good reviews. Maybe a DJ on a local station has expressed an interest. Maybe your music falls into a very specific genre – such as death metal, deep house, or progressive rock – which will make it easier and less expensive to market to a niche audience. Maybe the rejection letters you are receiving occasionally contain some encouraging comments. These are more positive and sound reasons for considering releasing your own records. At this stage, you need to ask yourself some serious questions.

- Do you really believe wholeheartedly in what you're doing?

- Does every member of the band have the same commitment as yourself?

- Are you prepared to invest potentially enormous amounts of work and money before you see a return?

- Are the other members of the band?

- Do you want to release your own records as a kind of exercise in vanity, just so that you can look at a CD with your name on it, or as a serious attempt to further your career?

- If you had a CD single or album right now would at least some people buy it?

- Is anyone other than friends or family telling you that your music is any good?

Hopefully you can answer positively to some or all of the above questions. If you can then you can begin to consider properly the implications of what you're getting yourself into. The attractions of signing a traditional record deal, especially a major deal, are obvious from the beginning. They mainly involve money, and the possibility of global distribution and ultimate fame. First, though, let's look a little closer at the reality.

a traditional record deal – the money

It's fair to say that any traditional record deal will involve some element of advance payment against the royalties which the artist will receive on record sales. So let's take the example of a band who sign a mid-level record deal, perhaps with a major label, and see how the figures stack up.

The first point to make is that most (if not all) payments made by record companies to artists are recoupable from the band's royalties. Some examples of recoupable payments are as follows:

advances

'Advances' traditionally means the recoupable payments made by a record company to an artist when the artist signs a deal, and then later when the artist delivers product (such as a single or an album) to the record company.

Later in the contract, further advances are paid when and if the record company exercises its contractual options to compel the band to make another album, and thus enter another contract period.

So what kind of money are we talking about? In the case of a band signing to a major record company on an average deal, the total advances in the so-called 'year one' of the deal may be, say, £60,000, with £30,000 payable on signature and £30,000 on delivery of the band's first album. £60,000 sounds like a fair chunk of money, but unfortunately the reality is far less exciting. The band will not simply be able to use the advances they receive for their own wages; at a bare minimum they will also have to pay their manager's commission and expenses and their accountant's fees. These are costs which it is up to the band to cover from their own funds, and do not involve the record company.

If we assume that we're talking about a four-piece band with a manager, who are also receiving an extra advance to buy some new equipment from the record company and even having their legal costs for signing the deal met by the record company as a recoupable cost, what is left divides out as follows:

Year One

Total advances £60,000

Less
    Management commission (20%) £12,000
    Management expenses (low estimate) £5,000
    Accountants fees (low estimate) £3,000

Remainder £40,000
Split four ways £10,000

Each band member receives £10,000

Perhaps the immediate impression that these figures create is that £10,000 per year (ie just under £200 per week) is actually a living wage. However, this assumes that a 'year' in the terms of the record contract is the same as a calendar year. In reality, it's sensible to assume that the first contract period under a recording contract is about 18 months. The reasons for this are many and varied, but it's unlikely that a band would be able to record, release and promote an album, tour it, and allow a record company enough time to evaluate whether it wishes to pick up the band's next option all within twelve short months.

So if we assume an 18-month first contract period, £10,000 works out at around £130 per week. Still okay, you may think – around £6,500 per year. However, you'll have to pay at least a small amount of tax and national insurance on that.

What if you happen to live in London? What if you were signing on, and are receiving housing benefit? Assuming that you would have to sign off, and that you could reclaim a certain amount of accommodation costs in government benefits, you're still looking at well under £75 a week to cover absolutely everything else, from bills and food and fags. Suddenly, signing a £60,000 record deal doesn't seem like the end of all your problems after all.

It would be a rosier picture if you were a solo artist, or part of a duo or three-piece band – the level of the advances isn't going to reduce on a curve, depending on how few members there are. But similarly, for a five-piece band, the advance isn't necessarily going to increase at all.

other recoupable costs

In addition to the advances paid by record companies to supposedly cover a band's living expenses and wages, the company will also pay for numerous other items which are recoupable from the band's royalties. These include:

(i) Recording Costs And Producer Fees

Normally, all recording costs and advances or fees paid by the record company to producers, remixers and engineers are recoupable. The term 'recording costs' covers everything from studio time to multitrack tapes, equipment hire, DATs, cabs home and food from the studio canteen. Every last item will go on the band's bill, including, for example, the cost of remixing tracks for overseas territories, which may never get released, and the costs of recording tracks which the company then rejects. The record company usually even recoups the cost of mastering the finished recordings.

Clearly, if artists and managers were in direct control of such costs then a much tighter rein would be kept on expenditure, unlike the actual reality, where the record company has *carte blanche* to spend its money on a band. If one assumes that a band records an album with a proper producer in moderate-to-expensive studios, and perhaps undertakes some remixing of tracks earmarked for singles, then it wouldn't be unusual for the recording costs incurred in year one to exceed £100,000. In addition, bands often undertake separate recording sessions for B-sides, demos or one-off tracks, which pushes the bill higher still.

tour support

This is the money which is advanced by the company to cover the shortfall on a tour budget, or to pay the 'buy-on' fees paid to a larger band in order to obtain the support slot on a tour. In addition to these costs, the record company may also agree to advance money for the purchase of equipment, as it's unlikely that any new band owns equipment good enough to withstand serious touring or playing on larger stages.

If touring is a significant part of the gameplan in the first year of a band's deal, tour support can add up to a high five-figure or even six-figure sum.

videos

Video is one area in which costs can spiral completely out of control. Assuming that a band releases, say, three singles in year one, each promotional video made by the record company can cost £15,000 or more, perhaps with an average of £25,000 – that's £75,000 spent on promo videos (which, incidentally, may never get shown), at least half of which is recoupable. It doesn't take a rocket scientist to work out that, if a record company spends £60,000 signing a band and incurs recoupable recording, tour support and video costs of the levels described above, the band's debit balance is already well over £300,000 – or roughly the cost of 20 terraced houses in Hull. Is it just me, or isn't that a massive amount of money spent to achieve, potentially, absolutely nothing?

But this is only half of the story. In addition to the recoupable costs spent by the record company, there are also heavy, non-recoupable costs which the record company has to front from its own funds. Some examples of these are manufacturing, distribution, marketing and promotion, administration and royalty accounting. Even if a record company baled out at the end of the first year (assuming that they had even bothered to release the band's album after a string of unsuccessful singles), it would not be uncommon for them to have spent over £500,000 in combined recoupable and non-recoupable costs.

£500,000! It's getting to the stage where you could almost buy Hull itself!

a traditional record deal – the people

Under the traditional scenario of signing a record deal, having a manager, an A&R man, a plugger and so on, it's fair to say that most bands would agree that they aren't in control of their career in any significant way. To some artists

– perhaps those that have signed a deal on the basis on some early demos, and without a few years of experience under their belts – the day-to-day realities of dealing with the people in the music business can be nightmarish.

At its most basic level, newly-signed artists are quickly aware that, for the first time, there are suddenly legions of people involved in their career who have strong opinions on their work, and – significantly – they are the very people who are controlling the work in the first place. Gone are the days when going into the studio was determined simply by whether the band could afford it or not. Instead, the record company will fund this, but only if an agreement is reached concerning which songs are to be recorded, who will produce them, which studio will be used, and when, and numerous conflicting opinions about what the finished tracks will sound like. It's extremely rare for newly-signed bands to be given anything like complete creative control.

On a whim, plans may change so that, instead of releasing the first single that all of the band want to be released, a completely different track may be substituted, at the behest of radio or TV influence. Videos may be shot and scrapped, and tracks may be remixed on the most bizarre pretexts. Different singles may also be released in different territories at the same time, for no apparent reason. Bands may find themselves at the mercy of a touring schedule which seems to have been put together by a madman, or they may find themselves kicking their heels at home with no gigs because touring suddenly seems vastly more expensive than it was just before they were signed. Gone are the days when gigging meant ringing up a club, piling the gear in the van, turning up and playing; now everything is part of strategy which may well make no sense whatsoever to the band.

In a worst-case scenario, the A&R guy who signed the band and was their champion within the company may move jobs or get fired, leaving the band at the mercy of his or her successor, who may well want to clear the decks completely. Alternatively, the company may hit problems, get taken over, or merge. You may have signed the deal with dreams of stardom, of becoming the biggest band in the world, only for the reality of the situation to be cruelly disappointing.

Allow yourself to imagine that you were in such a band. You've signed your record deal, recorded your album, made some videos and been on tour. Maybe a few other territories have decided to release the album. Maybe you've been on TV a few times, and everyone in your town knows that you're in that band that got that big record deal last year. You've been living on your £75-a-week wages and have been tantalisingly close to the rock 'n' roll dream. Close, but sadly no cigar.

Instead, 18 months down the line you've been dropped by the record company owing £350,000 on your debit, which has no chance of ever recouping as your album has already been deleted. You've fallen out with your manager, you can't afford to tour without the record company's support, and your fans think you've disappeared off the face of the Earth.

There are two possible approaches to take at this point: one is to decide that it was fun while it lasted, you had a good laugh and an adventure, and the real world had been put on hold for a while; the other is to rue the fact that you had no control over your own destiny, and that the copyright in your creative work is now owned by a bunch of idiots in a skyscraper in New York. It may be that your hopes of a long and fruitful career in music have been irreparably hindered. Finally, you may realise that you've worked your arse off for years to no avail, on less wages than you would earn delivering leaflets for three days a week.

The point of all this ranting is to ask one very simple question: do you really want a traditional record deal to the exclusion of all else, or do you just want to get your records out? If it's the latter, read on.

doing it yourself – the pros and cons

Very briefly, the perceived disadvantages of the DIY approach can be summarised as follows:

i) Lack Of Enough Money To Make A Significant Impact

Obviously, hardly anybody has the same amount of cash lying around to spend on their career as a major record company, so you'll have to cut your cloth accordingly. It's surprising what can be achieved for a modest outlay, however, as long as you remember that the overall plan is to actually make money rather than simply spend it. With careful budgeting (and assuming that a certain amount of favours can be pulled), it has probably never been cheaper in real terms to record, manufacture and promote a finished product.

It's a fact that record companies – or major companies, at least – waste vast amounts of money on calculated risks that may well not pay off: a hugely-expensive tour may produce nowhere near the extra sales necessary to cover the costs of mounting it; a promotional video may be made at great expense and never seen. In you choose to take the DIY approach, your task is to make every penny you spend count – in other words, every expense must be tied to direct income or direct and conclusive advancement of your career.

ii) Hard Work And Administration

There is no doubt that there is a huge amount of hard work involved in setting up any new business, and going it alone in the music industry is no exception. However, bands who sign major record deals work equally hard, albeit in a different environment and possibly for less reward at the end of the day. The major difference is that the signed band rarely has any choice of when and where to work, and life – particularly that of a pop artist – is an endless round of press and promotion. This may sound great, but the reality is much less glamorous; after all, would anyone really want to get up at 5am on a Saturday morning to be interviewed by a puppet? In any case, you must remind yourself that this route is not open to you, at least at present.

The fine detail of artwork, manufacturing and promotion may be a boring subject, but perhaps the best way to deal with it is to accept that, if your hard work pays off, you'll get to keep the money you make. And you'll also still own your recordings.

perception

Clearly, the band from your home town who have just signed to Virgin are going to make a bit more of a splash than the guys who are putting out their own record. The independent route is certainly rather lonely, and there's a feeling of existing in a vacuum. This mainly arises from not having a huge team of people around you telling you how great you are 24 hours a day. In time, however, direct contact with your audience (and, more specifically, direct sales to them) will certainly be more meaningful. After all, labels controlled by artists – or, at least, perceived to be controlled by artists – aren't exactly a new thing: Oasis have emerged from the closure of Creation with their own label, Big Brother, which is licensed through Sony, and the Beatles did the same thing with Apple.

The perceived difference is that these bands have become hugely successful under traditional contractual arrangements and have then used their new bargaining power to strike the kind of restructured deals they want. However, artists like Ani di Franco have been selling their own product for years by not attempting to emulate the approach of the majors, and selling millions of albums in the process. In other words, plenty of artists have taken the pro-active route of deciding that they don't want a traditional record deal.

The key is to treat the DIY approach as simply a sensible step in extending and promoting your own career as an artist. Who knows what may happen a few releases down the line? The industry may be beating a path to your door by then, and you may be able to pick and choose with whom you work, or you may even decide to remain independent. Surely it's better to take matters into your own hands than to simply keep shoving new demo tapes in the post, waiting for the almost inevitable thumbs down? It's a sad fact that nobody owes you a career, or indeed a living. Even if you're genuinely one of the most exciting and original artists of recent years, there's no point sitting around, waiting for record companies to wake up to your talents.

control

Control has a broad sweep of implications for any artist. At its most basic, it means that you have the freedom to call the band what you like, to look how you like, to record the songs you like and to release as many or as few as you like – budget permitting, of course. On a deeper level, it means owning and controlling your own copyrights, whether they are recordings or songs, and deciding how and when they are exploited. Assuming that the entire intrinsic value of the music industry is based on the ownership of rights, then clearly the ideal situation is to possess your own. Even if you wish to license them, perhaps to an overseas company, such deals should ideally be arranged on a short-term basis, which will ensure the return of your rights within a few years.

Control also applies to what you do and when. It would be impossible, for example, to retain a regular or even part-time job after being signed to a traditional record deal. (Indeed, some people might class this as an advantage.) Signed bands aren't in control of their own schedules, particularly in relation to promotion and touring. Under your own steam, however, you'll be able to construct a sensible and achievable strategy by which to further your career, rather than complying with numerous different agendas, which are ultimately unlikely to have your band's best interests at heart.

income

As we will see later in this book, the potential income to be derived from selling your music directly far outweighs the income that bands receive under a traditional record deal by way of royalties. In addition, this higher income is received far more regularly than the average record company's six-monthly royalty statement.

conclusion

It's too glib to suggest that all artists looking to take control of their product and career should take the DIY approach, and that they would derive a higher level of income than they would otherwise. Clearly there are many aspects of a traditional record deal that are appealing, and it's too easy to paint a picture of record companies as evil capitalist monsters bent on exploiting artists and their recordings. However, if you assume that the record company route isn't open to you, it's important take the DIY approach with the right motivation, and look at the advantages. If you start releasing your own records with the feeling that it runs a very poor second to signing a record deal then you're scuppered before you start. Accentuate the positive, and concentrate on the advantages you are about to enjoy. After all, you can't drop yourself.

chapter 2

setting up

Once you have decided to go ahead and release your own records, you need to proceed in much the same way as anyone entering into a new business venture, whether as a sole trader or through a limited company. However, there are a few key areas relating to the way in which your business becomes established and begins to trade which are unique to the music industry and any other creative industry which deals in the sale of copyrights.

It's important to stress that, although the product you will eventually be selling is derived from unique creative endeavour, the business of selling and promoting that product most be approached in a businesslike fashion, in the same way as running a corner shop or being a door-to-door salesman. Clearly starting up is slightly different for everyone, so for the purpose of this chapter we will assume that we are dealing with a five-piece band, one of whom writes all the songs, with the rest of the band contributing to the arrangement of the music. We will thus be dealing with the exploitation (by which we effectively mean the distribution and sale) of two types of copyright entities – songs, and recordings. First, though, it's important to understand the difference between a song and a recording, as this is an area which can lead to some confusion.

songs

The song itself, by which we mean the music and lyrics, is the entity which is being recorded, and the copyright in that song is owned by either the songwriter, or songwriters, or to whomever the songwriter(s) have decided to assign their copyright in the song, such as a publishing company.

The importance of establishing the ownership of the songs to be recorded at a very early stage cannot be emphasised enough. In particular, it's important to be aware that the owners of the copyright in songs are entitled to receive payments when such songs are mechanically reproduced (ie pressed on CD or duplicated in some other way), performed (ie on the radio or live), or exploited in various other ways (ie being used on a TV programme or in a film). The significance of this is that, should you decide to record your version of a song written by somebody else, you'll need to make provision to pay that songwriter or their publisher the sums to which they are entitled on any pressings of the album or single that you sell.

For the time being, however, let's assume that the band in question intend to record only their own material. At this point, it's both sensible and prudent to have a clear agreement within the band concerning the individual shares of the members in the songs in question. In practical terms, such an agreement isn't likely to be controversial, as bands invariably discuss who wrote what from time to time. There is no set formula which can be used to fit every situation, but by using our example of the five-piece band with one principle writer, a fair solution might be as follows.

Assuming that the principle writer attends rehearsals with the songs he has written, including the lyrics, then it's likely that, in the course of the whole band learning and discussing the songs, certain minor changes may be made. For example, the odd lyric here or there may be altered if one of the band suggests something better, or a chord may change from being major to minor. The rhythm of the song may be tried in a number of different ways before the best version is agreed on. All of these changes can be grouped together under the practise of 'arranging' the song, in a particularly loose sense of the word. In this case, it might be fair that the main songwriter agrees that the whole band (including himself or herself) has a share of the song (20% altogether, for example, or in other words 4% each) allocated to them which reflects their contribution to the arrangement.

In many cases, such an agreed split does not give the other contributors a recognised share in the copyright in the song. The arrangement is purely financial, with the principle songwriter agreeing to put 20% of any income that arises into an 'arrangement pot', which all of the band members band can share. In other words, the songwriter won't expect to be restricted in his usage of the song in the future (for example, if he or she succeeded in striking a publishing deal), even if this particular project or band founders.

Anyone who followed the recent court case between some of the former members of Spandau Ballet will be aware that the division of the songwriting spoils in any band is one of the most common causes of resentment and confusion between band members. Some bands (notably Blur) are well known for succeeding in avoiding any such antagonism by simply splitting songwriting revenues equally between them, which is highly unusual. However, this approach does have the benefit of avoiding the possibility of making a lot of lawyers rich at some future point and, perhaps more sadly in the case of Spandau Ballet, washing a band's dirty linen in the glare of the media spotlight.

In most cases, then, it's far more prudent to have a clear agreement between the members of a band regarding the ownership of the songs in question, especially before time and money is spent recording and releasing them. Such an agreement can be drafted quite easily by a specialist music business solicitor, and in this situation it's probably unnecessary for each member of the band to obtain separate legal advice. However, the agreement must reflect in writing that all of the signatories have taken such specialist legal advice, or there will be a danger that some of the band may claim that they didn't understand what they were agreeing at the time. The percentage split can hopefully be agreed amicably, in advance of instructing a lawyer, which will save time.

protecting the copyright in songs

It's extremely sensible to take some simple steps to establish ownership of the copyright in songs, particularly if those songs are about to be recorded and distributed. Without going into an exhaustive explanation of copyright issues, a songwriter may be required to prove ownership of a song in case of a dispute involving unauthorised usage or plagiarism. There are a number of simple and cheap methods which can be used to establish the authorship of songs at a given date. For example, the writer can place a cassette of song demos and/or music and lyric sheets in a sealed envelope and post them to himself by registered post, leaving the package unopened when it arrives and retaining the registered posting documentation. Alternatively, the same package can be dated and countersigned by a witness (preferably a professional, such as a doctor, accountant or, best of all, a solicitor) and deposited with them for safekeeping.

Once the copyright ownership in the songs has been established and agreed in writing, and the writer(s) have protected their copyright, then the recordings themselves can be dealt with.

recordings

Under the Copyright, Designs And Patents Act of 1988, the owner of the copyright in a recording is defined as the person who made the arrangements whereby such a recording came to be created. In traditional record deals this would be the record company, although there is currently a school of thought that insists that the record producers themselves are involved in the authorship of copyright, even if hired by the record company. For the purposes of this book, however, it's assumed that the band are paying for their own recording costs and hiring the studio engineer to do no more than engineer the sessions for them as part of their deal with the studio. As such, the band themselves are producing the sessions, and creating and owning the copyrights in the recordings. Yet who are the band, in this instance?

At this point, some hard questions need to be asked about the nature of the band members' business relationships with each other. Effectively, most new and unsigned bands tend to have one or two members who are the leaders, or perhaps the founders of the band, and who are the motivating force behind the band. In business terms, most bands are operating as a kind of equal partnership; it's a rare event for a new and unsigned band to be run by a limited company, in which all of the band members were involved as directors. Such an arrangement might make sense in the future – for tax purposes, as well as to limit liability – but not at this stage.

In basic terms, if all of the members of the band contribute equally to the costs of recording the tracks in question then the copyright in those recordings is owned jointly by the band, as a kind of partnership. If everything proceeds smoothly then this approach is fine; difficulties only arise if, for example, one member of the band leaves. It's vital to ensure that there are no restrictions on the exploitation (ie sale and distribution) of the recordings created by the band, whatever the circumstances. In practice, if the lead singer leaves the band as soon as the recordings are completed, they are effectively useless unless the multitrack tapes are retained and his replacement can revocal the tracks.

The only way to be absolutely clear about the ownership and eventual use of the recordings is to draw up a simple partnership agreement between all of the band members. This will be similar to the above agreement, in which the songwriting splits are stated, but this agreement deals only with the recordings themselves. In essence, the agreement needs to reflect the following:

- That all of the members of the band are contributing to the cost of the recordings, and jointly own the copyright in such recordings

- That it's agreed that the purpose of making the recordings is to exploit them commercially, and to promote the career of the band

- That any income derived from the exploitation of the recordings will first be used to repay each contributor to the costs of the recordings in equal instalments (or *pro rata*)

- That if the band/partnership splits up, or if any member of the band/partnership leaves, then the recordings may still be exploited in any manner upon which that the majority of the joint owners agree, subject to the split of income remaining as before.

Such an agreement should be contained in a general partnership agreement between all band members, and the conditions in it could apply equally well to income derived from sales of merchandise and so on. The key point is that the band partnership agreement should not concern songwriting credits, ownership and usage at all; it should reflect the fact that the band, as a band, is likely to generate income from main areas such as record sales, merchandising and touring, and split such income in agreed proportions between the members of the band.

Songwriting or publishing income is a matter only for the songwriters in the band, unless it has been agreed that the band should participate in songwriting income equally, whatever the actual songwriting credits. Even if this were the case, it would be unwise to reflect such an arrangement in the main band partnership agreement: a separate agreement should be constructed. The reason for this is that bands (and band members) come and go, but songs exist forever.

Although it may seem faintly ridiculous to delve into the nitty gritty of drafting partnership agreements before the band had even got its recording career under way, it's best to start as you mean to go on. Imagine, if you will, that Oasis had recorded a mini album at their own expense before they got signed, but in the interim period one or more members of that particular line-up of the band had been sacked, or they left of their own accord: such a mini album would be worth a fortune, especially if it contained early versions of songs which were later re-recorded and became huge hits. The ownership of such a recordings would be an extremely important issue, and one which would possibly become the subject of legal proceedings, so having the paperwork in order would be an enormous advantage in establishing true ownership and exploitation rights.

To recap, then, there are three areas that concern the internal workings of any band before they embark on their recording career: who are the writers of the songs which are being considered for recording, and what split of ownership and income in respect of these songs is agreed between the relevant parties; in respect of recordings, who will own the copyright in such recordings and the right to exploit them commercially, and what split of income is agreed between these owners; that the band is likely to need a brief and simple partnership agreement, determining the way in which they will conduct their business.

partnership agreements

Some form of partnership agreement is highly desirable, if not vital, before a band starts spending money on its career. Such an agreement serves to ensure that all members of a band are fully aware of the business into which they are entering together, and that there are no misunderstandings that will come back to haunt them later.

In essence, the band will be forming a partnership for the purposes of furthering their careers as recording and performing music artists. The agreement will reflect the split of income that has been agreed between the band on the exploitation of the recordings, of that earned by performing live. It will also deal with issues such as who is to control the partnership bank account, and what restrictions there are upon this, as well as the ownership of recordings, artwork, and the band name and logo. It's also useful to agree upon what will happen if one or more members of the band decide to leave, and who is entitled to carry on using the band name in that event.

do you need a lawyer?

The short answer is yes, but with some qualifications. Any band which intends to start releasing recordings and dealing with the music business needs to retain the services of a solicitor who specialises in the music business. However, this isn't to say that any competent non-music solicitor wouldn't be able to put together a simple partnership agreement of the kind described above. Essentially, the partnership agreement will be very similar to that drafted for any group of individuals who wish to go into business together. There may be some difficulty in explaining to the non-music lawyer the difference between songs and recordings, but on the whole the main partnership agreement is a relatively simple document.

When it comes to dealing with specific areas within the music business, such as licensing, distribution and publishing, there is no option but to use a specialist music solicitor. Indeed, many of the companies with which you may end up dealing will insist that you warrant that you have taken specialist legal advice before they enter into an agreement with you.

Music business solicitors tend to be much removed from the traditional image of the lawyer, and retaining their services should not be seen as a worrying matter. They are there to help you and fight your corner. Many solicitors will offer a free initial consultation, in which you can discuss with them what you need to achieve, or a deal you have been offered. If you don't have much money to spend you should be completely open with the solicitor because, once they begin to work for you, their fees can range from £150 to over £300 per hour, plus costs. However, many music business firms have junior solicitors and legal executives, who will provide more affordable advice and work for clients with a smaller budget. The logic for this is that the client will hopefully move onto bigger and better things, earning a more substantial revenue, and the firm will then begin to be able to charge its more standard fees.

Music business solicitors also fill another non-legal role, in that they will be a source of industry gossip and contacts, perhaps suggesting that a client of theirs who is a record label, or a distributor for whom they act, may be interested in your material. They may also have other bands as clients whom you may be able to approach in order to obtain support slots, or they may act for producers and studios who may also be useful contacts for you.

For new clients, it is almost always the case that a solicitor will ask for some money on account before he or she commences work, and you should be prepared for this. You should also be aware that, if you phone your solicitor on a regular basis and take up their time, you will get a bill unless you have specifically agreed on a friendly basis that you may call up every so often and ask a few questions.

Many artists fall into the trap of thinking that, if they retain the services of an expensive music business solicitor, they have advanced their career enormously. This is not the case in the UK, although in America lawyers are much more pro-active in touting their clients around the business. You should look at hiring a music business solicitor as an expense that is as necessary as studio time in your new business.

finances

Assuming that you've decided to establish a partnership through which to conduct the band's business, the next step is to bring in an accountant to handle the partnership's financial affairs and deal with issues such as tax and VAT. This may sound slightly over the top to a band who have just decided to press ahead and make their own records, but sound financial advice is vital, even at an early stage.

Many accountants will offer new clients a free initial consultation, and it's less vital that an accountant is specifically expert in the music business than it is when appointing a solicitor to act for the band. You should expect to provide your accountant with details of your current employment so that he can explain the tax implications of operating as a partnership while at the same time perhaps some or all of the band are employed under the PAYE scheme.

It may be sensible for the partnership to register for VAT if there are likely to be significant expenses that include VAT which can be recovered. VAT registration is compulsory if it is expected that the partnership may turn over in excess of £50,000 in any one year. Be aware, however, that, although you will be able to reclaim VAT on expenses that you are charged by third parties, you will also have to pay the VAT that you charge within the price of the goods you sell. In other words, if you sell and album for £12 and you are VAT registered, then 17.5% (the current VAT rate) of that price (about £1.80) will have to be paid over to the VAT man. However, if you incur costs in studio time, mastering and manufacturing, which have VAT added to them, you will be able to recover the tax element. On balance, it is probably unnecessary to register for VAT if a relatively modest turnover is expected; the cost in accountancy fees of preparing quarterly VAT returns may outweigh any benefits you may gain by reclaiming VAT in the first place.

Opening a bank account for the partnership may be more difficult than you might imagine, particularly if you approach a bank or building society that has had no dealings with any members of the band before now. Some banks insist on seeing a full business plan for any new venture before they will consider opening an account, and it's fair to say that the traditional high street banks take a somewhat jaundiced view of any music-business-related activity. It may be simpler to open a business account, or perhaps what is known as a treasurer's account (ie one designed for clubs and societies) at a local building society. You're unlikely to get a cheque book, at least at first, but counter cheques can be issued if necessary over the counter.

Delegating one member of the band to be responsible for finances can be an area of some difficulty, not because it involves any lack of trust but simply because it's not a particularly exciting area to look after. Somebody needs to draw the short straw, however, and be the person who keeps a record of all expenses and receipts, credits all income to the account, and liaises with the accountant when required. It's clearly desirable to have some restrictions built in to control the band's finances, and it should perhaps be agreed that no bills should be paid unless they have been signed off by at least two members of the band/partners.

It's probably unnecessary to have more than one bank account for each of the bands' potential sources of income (record sales, merchandise sales and gigs), as to do so will probably incur extra bank charges and administration. However, it's important to ensure that proper management accounts are kept for each area, so that their profitability (or otherwise) can be easily assessed.

No business can start without at least a small investment to get things up and running and provide a float in the account. It's therefore sensible for each member of the band to credit the same amount to the account, which will be reflected as "working capital introduced" in the partnership accounts. In other words, before any profits for the partnership can be assessed, such working capital can be refunded to the partners if required.

Most band members have completely different financial circumstances. Some will be working but have little or no spare cash, and some may be signing on but have a nest egg in the bank. As money is one of the main areas of dispute in bands, it's as well to deal with this from the very beginning. If one or more members of the band is able to contribute more than the rest (perhaps temporarily), it's infinitely preferable that such contribution should be approached in the following way.

Rather than the slightly haphazard situation in which each member of the band turns up at rehearsals or recording with their own small contribution, it's much better to have all such funds paid into the band's bank account and to meet expenses with a band cheque or band cash. In this way a receipt can be given to the partnership, and it will also be possible to avoid disputes about who has paid their contribution and who hasn't. This will make things much easier for the person in charge of finance, and will reduce the time the accountant has to spend sorting out myriad receipts. It will also make it easy to calculate how much each partner/band member is owed at any time.

It's sensible to make the name of the account the same as that of the band itself, although in reality the account name is likely to be "Name Of Band Member(s) T/A (Trading As) Name Of Band". In the event that only one member of the band is able to open the account, it must be established straight away with the band accountant that this person is effectively acting as a nominee for the whole band, and not receiving the income personally.

Partnership accounts should be prepared by the accountant on an annual basis, and the partnership will have to pay tax on any profits, as well as on any drawings (ie wages) taken by the partners.

limited companies

It would be surprising if an accountant recommended the formation of a limited company to handle the business affairs of a new or fledgling band.

Companies cost a significant amount of money to form and administer, and the accounting procedures required for a company are more onerous (and therefore more expensive) than for a partnership. With a limited company, the accountant would probably suggest that all members of the band became directors and equal shareholders. The advantage of conducting business through a limited company is that it restricts personal liability in the event that any losses are incurred, or if the company is embroiled in a legal dispute.

On the whole, unless the band is likely to turn over a considerable amount of money straight away, or is intending to carry out business in areas in which limited liability may be useful, forming a company is probably too expensive and cumbersome to be a sensible option.

the band's name

The key issues here are: what is the band name, and is anyone else using it?; who currently owns the name – the whole band, or certain members?; and is it sensible to consider a change in name now that the band is going to release its own product? It's relatively easy to establish whether or not the name of your is unique. Apart from contacting organisations such as The Bands Register (see appendices), searching the web should also unearth any other bands of any commercial significance which are using the same name. Try searching not only sites such as iMusic (www.imusic.com) but also CD retailers such as Amazon and CDNow, and the sites of music publications. A trawl around large record stores and their catalogues – especially stores that deal in imports as well as UK product – is also recommended.

If you find a band which has released product that has the same name, or one so similar that it is potentially problematic, you should seriously consider changing your the name of your band. The fact that you have been using the name for longer, or are better known in your area, is moot; confusion doesn't help in any way. If you accept that the music business is becoming globally more accessible with every passing day, it therefore follows that, if a band in Baltimore or Bangkok is releasing product under the same name as your band, they have got there first. You may be in a position to offer your product for international licensing or export in the very near future, and their product may be already being imported into the UK.

As long as your band's name is clean, you should register it with The Bands Register immediately, and establish a web site for the band. This subject will be covered later in this book.

Ownership of bands' names is a thorny topic, and has been the subject of numerous disputes over the years, particularly on the live circuit, where bands have toured with members who have only the flimsiest of connections with the line-up of the band people have paid money to see. Band names have often been owned by the management company, and in some cases by the record company itself, rather than by the individual band members.

Your partnership agreement should clearly reflect who owns the name of the band, and – in the event of one or more members leaving – who, if anyone, will be entitled to carry on using the name. The agreement may provide that any member of the band who leaves may be allowed to refer to the band's name on gig advertising for their new band (as in 'ex-Purple Couches'), but only on the basis that the original band's name is in a smaller typeface than the ex-member's new band. Discussion of band name ownership is often uncomfortable, especially if, like most bands, there is one or more founder member who feels that they own the name. However, if the band is about to begin formally releasing its own product, things have stepped up a gear and it's necessary to delve into some difficult areas and reach agreement.

A new name needs to be memorable, unique, and as short as possible, . The last point is purely a practical one – in terms of artwork for posters and inlay cards, the shorter the name the more striking it can be. Even bands such as Fun Lovin' Criminals regularly shorten their poster artwork to FLC in order to get the message across in as large type as possible.

You should resist the temptation to make the band name too controversial, jokey, elaborate or pretentious. Make sure that the name is easily pronounceable in as many languages as possible (or when drunk!), is easy to spell, and is difficult to mishear. Avoid using any name which is connected to a company, product or prominent individual. Assume that people are unable to spell even the simplest word, and you won't go far wrong. Whatever name you select, you'll get used to it in a week. I'm not sure why – it just always seems to take a week.

So let's see how far we've come by the time we reach this point. You now have a list of all the songs which are potentially in the frame to be recorded. You have agreed on the ownership of the songs, and/or the split of songwriters income, in writing, and the ownership of the songs is protected as much as is possible. The band now has a partnership agreement, setting out the aims of the business, the finances and income split, leaving-member provisions, ownership of the band name and logo, and the ownership of recordings. There is now a band accountant and a band bank account, and a member of the band has been delegated to take care of financial matters.

The band now also has a solicitor, who has drafted the partnership agreement, which has been signed by all the members of the band. The name of the band is agreed, and there is an appropriate logo designed.

These are all the basic nuts and bolts which are required to establish a firm bedrock upon which to proceed. At first glance they all seem more than a little dull and boring, but they are all very necessary; too many bands drift along for too long without handling their affairs in a businesslike way, concentrating solely on the creative side.

All of these areas concentrate on the internal workings of the band as a business. The next stage is to look at how the band interacts with the outside world, and how this can be improved from the very beginning.

communications

At its most basic level, where are the band and how will they communicate with their audience and the business? Most bands would love to have their own dedicated rehearsal space, office, phone line and so on, but finances tend to rule this out. However, there are a couple of changes that can be made in order to present a more businesslike image.

Headed paper is essential. This should include the band's logo, although it need not be elaborate. If there is any doubt that the address of the band is less than permanent, you should consider using a PO box, from which you can either collect mail from or have delivered to you. Remember that, if you release a CD with an address on it, that CD may be in circulation for a considerable amount of time before somebody decides that they want to get in touch with the band. In terms of a phone number, it may be wise to invest in a 'number for life', which can be diverted to wherever your band ends up, or even to a mobile or voicemail. You should also get some basic business cards printed, which include the band's logo, their address, contact details, and their website address. These can be incredibly useful when doing the rounds of the local music scene, and will lend the band the air of professionals.

A fax machine – even a basic £100 model – is pretty much an essential piece of equipment. If you can afford a plain paper model then so much the better, because thermal paper machines are unwieldly and the paper fades quickly. It's important that the band's details change as little as possible, once you've started to communicate with the outside world. Therefore, hook the fax machine up to a number that is unlikely to change for the foreseeable future, rather than one in a rented flat or other temporary accommodation. You might even consider using the fax machine at your regular rehearsal space, if you get on well with the people there and can trust them to pass faxes on to you.

If you have access to a PC then this can also help, although preferably use your own rather than one you borrow. E-mail is becoming an essential tool of business, and people certainly tend to respond to emails much faster than phone calls. The ideal situation would be to register the band's name as your domain name. Any self-respecting band should really have their own website, however basic, and this will be discussed in more detail later in this book.

trading style

A certain amount of ingenuity and front needs to be employed when deciding how to present the band to the outside world. In many cases the band will want to write to and fax people under the band's name and on band headed paper. However, it is not sensible to use the same approach for the band's releases, for reasons of perception. It's far better if communications regarding the band's releases appear to be coming from a record label, rather than from the band itself. The label in question should of course not simply be the band's name followed by the word 'Records', as this would give the game away. Pick a completely different label name, and – in the same way as the band name – make as many enquiries as possible to ensure that it isn't already being used.

This ruse may seem elaborate and unnecessary, but it works. If you were a journalist, or a radio researcher, and you received a package from a band – let's call them Sanctuary – on 'Sanctuary' headed paper, including a CD which had a 'Sanctuary Records' logo on it, the overall effect would be underwhelming, to say the least. It simply suggests that here was some local band that had put their own record out. (The truth, in other words.) If, on the other hand, they receive a letter from 'XYZ Records' or whatever, along with a Sanctuary CD and biography, then the presumption arises that maybe this is a more authentic release, as the band clearly have a record company behind them. Don't forget that numerous indie labels – some of them well known and highly credible – amount to little more than one person, a phone and a filing cabinet.

I don't mind admitting that I have used this ruse successfully on a couple of occasions when I've been managing bands that have released their own records. It can make a lot of difference (depending on who you're calling at the time) to appear to be from a record company rather than just the band's manager. Similarly, when plugging a record to radio yourself without being able to afford the services of a professional plugger, people receive it differently if a they think that a band's single has been sent to them by a plugging or PR company. More of that later.

By this stage you have obtained the following things to assist you in dealing with the world outside: an address or PO box number for the band, permanent phone and fax numbers, and an email address; headed paper for the band, containing the band's logo and all of the above details; business cards; a 'label' identity for the band, with a logo and headed paper, containing the same contact details as above but perhaps with an email address (making sure that this doesn't involve the band's name); and a website. So what else do you need?

biography

Every artist needs a biography, however flimsy, to inform people who they are, what they have done, what they are going to do, and when and why they are going to do it. Whilst every effort should be made to write biographies that are entertaining and informative, it's better to err on the side of brevity and fact rather than to generate page after page of boring rambling about the band, or to blatantly lie. The way a biography reads is stylistically very important, and it may be a good idea to borrow heavily from the language of the weekly music press. So a one-page biography for our heroes, Sanctuary, should look something like this:

SANCTUARY
(band logo)
Biog: June 2000

Pete Rimadonna – lead vocals; Les Paul – guitars, vocals;
Billy Nomates – keyboards; Mick Shrimpton – drums; Hugo Furst – bass

SANCTUARY formed in mid 1999 from the ashes of Sheffield's favourite sons, Quasimodo, once tipped to follow Pulp and Def Leppard as the Next Big Thing from South Yorkshire.

After releasing a highly-acclaimed debut EP on Pie Records at the tail end of 1998, Quasimodo split shortly afterwards, leaving their legions of followers to wonder what might have been. Well wonder no more.

Original Quasimodo lead vocalist Pete Rimadonna has teamed up with ex-Spotweld guitarist Les Paul to form **SANCTUARY**. Recruiting original Quasimodo rhythm section Mick Shrimpton and Hugo Furst, together with previously-unknown keyboard wizard Billy Nomates, Sanctuary have burst onto the live circuit with a vengeance.

Critics have already described **SANCTUARY** as "the bastard sons of Supergrass and Happy Mondays", a fitting indication of the explosive mix of influences which make

SANCTUARY something special. Instantly danceable songs, combined with explosive choruses, spiky guitars, topped off with Rimadonna's trademark wounded vocals.

SANCTUARY are currently preparing to record their debut mini album, scheduled for release in the autumn. In the meantime, the band are playing a series of dates around the North, as well as occasional shows in London in front of an ever-growing number of industry admirers.

For further details, contact: (band details)

So not a gigantic amount of information has been expanded upon to construct a provocative and (hopefully) entertaining biography which basically says little more than that a new band has formed. Note also that the band's name always appears in bold type to add emphasis. The band's biography needs to be updated regularly to add significant new information, and should always be included whenever the band issue a new press release.

press release

Supplying the local and national press with information is a vital part of projecting the band's businesslike image. It's therefore important that regular press releases are issued for the purposes of notifying the press of forthcoming gigs, releases, or to provide stories about the band even when there is no hard news.

Most press releases will be issued to inform the press about gigs, and for this it's vital to include as much information as possible in order to make the journalist's job easier. Even if you're playing at the only club in town, you should still always put down the address, phone number, door times, ticket prices and support bands. A press release from Sanctuary might look something like this:

SANCTUARY
(band logo)

SANCTUARY emerge from the studio next month to play a one-off date at Club Toilette.

The show will see the debut of some new material and a sneak preview of some of the tracks from the band's forthcoming mini-album.

SANCTUARY bass player Hugo Furst will be celebrating his safe return to the UK after being savaged by a rabid badger on a recent camping holiday in the Pyrenees.

Support comes from Hull-based grindcore merchants Savage Haddock.

Date:	Saturday July 4th
Venue:	Club Toilette @ the Rat & Kebab, 31 Pit Street, Sheffield
	Tel: 02765 2975386
Doors Open:	7.30pm
Support:	Savage Haddock (onstage 9pm)
Headline:	**SANCTUARY** (onstage 10pm)
Tickets:	£4 advance, £5 door. Advance tickets available from Tumbleweed Records in the Arndale Centre.
Notes:	Under 18s not admitted

See over for **SANCTUARY** biography.

The point about putting the hopefully amusing (and clearly totally fabricated) story about the bass player in there is that it will provide a jaded journalist with something light hearted to spice up an otherwise dull press release.

You should get into the habit of issuing regular press releases, and making sure that each one contains new information, in addition to the main news within it. Clearly, one member of the band will need to be delegated with the job of communicating with the outside world, and ensuring that the band's biography is up to date. This is a fairly administratively-intensive task, but at least not as boring as being in charge of the accounts.

press details

The band should immediately build up a database of local and national music journalists, containing their direct phone and fax numbers, email addresses if possible, and postal addresses. The aim should be to establish a good rapport with all local music journalists straight away, whether they write a weekly column for the local paper or for fanzines and student magazines. Journalists thrive on information, and the more professionally you present yourselves the more coverage you are likely to get.

It isn't vital that all journalists love the band, as a large part of their reporting is purely factual, and they are also duty-bound to provide their readers with wide coverage of the local music scene. However, it never does any harm to befriend journalists, and always put them on the guest list, at the very least. In terms of the national press, both the *NME* and *Melody Maker* still provide comprehensive gig listings, and you should be prepared to send them details of every date you play. Be warned that they will ask you for details of what the band sounds like, the phone number of the venue and other information; if you don't provide them with this, they won't print the information.

The more you can do by email the cheaper and more efficient it will be, particularly as far as publication deadlines are concerned. You should be aware of the deadlines for all local papers and fanzines, and work backwards from the date of your gig to establish the latest possible time that you can submit information. Also, certain journalists may be prepared or able to use the band's logo in their articles, so for this purpose it's useful to have some spare disks handy which contain different versions of the logo.

band photograph

An official band photograph which fulfils a variety of purposes is absolutely vital. Generally speaking, the most effective band shots are those which are striking, slightly weird, and which concentrate on the bands faces, or at least their top halves. Photos which have a full-length band shot tend to look insignificant when reduced down to the size of a postcard or flyer.

Scan the music press for shots of bands that catch your eye and try for something similar, but disregard the live shots as these aren't really ideal for what you need. You may be able to find a professional photographer with a studio setup, or a photography student with access to good equipment who will shoot the band for the cost of the film and printing, or at least at a very low budget. Music photography is an area that many amateur and semi-professional photographers are eager to enter. You should meet with the photographer to discuss shots of other bands that you like, whilst remembering that (if the photographer is working for you as a favour) it's best to also humour his or her own ideas, some of which may work out better than your own.

Once you have decided to go ahead with a photo session, you'll need to think seriously about how you want the band to look. The shot you select is likely to be around to haunt you for some considerable time, so choosing the right look for the band right is very important. Although every musical genre is different, it's hard to go wrong with a very understated and timeless look, dressed down rather than dressed up. It's unwise to emulate the style and image of artists you admire, who have spent thousands of pounds on one photo session, as your attempts are likely to look second rate in comparison. You should also avoid a shot which looks too gimmicky, which journalists are likely to get bored with very quickly and stop using. Many local papers will now only use colour shots, and so it's sensible to ensure that the session is a mixture of colour and black-and-white shots.

For the session itself, it's a good idea to turn up with a variety of different outfits and be prepared to swap clothes with each other if necessary. Don't be afraid of using make-up to mask any blemishes, either – everyone does it, and it's likely for it to be undetectable on the final shot. I would caution against taking any shots with your instruments, however, as this kind of shot now looks indescribably cheesy. Unless you're used to attending photo sessions, if you're uncomfortable with any pose suggested by the photographer then your discomfort is probably going to show, so don't waste time on setups with which you aren't happy. Also, you should make sure that there are some individual shots taken of each member of the band.

Once the session is complete, ask the photographer to provide a contact sheet (ie a sheet of negative-sized prints) of all of the photographs that have been taken, and examine them carefully with a magnifying glass, crossing out shots which are totally unusable, before coming up with a shortlist of potential candidates. One useful tip is to look carefully at everyone's eyeline in the shots comprising the final shortlist – because the contact sheet is so small, it's very easy to miss a shot in which someone is looking slightly awry, or blinking. It's sensible to choose at least two or three final shots to be printed and duplicated; in this way you can provide local journalists with a choice of shot if they (or their editor) get bored with continually using the same one.

flyers

With a bit of forethought and ingenuity, band flyers can fulfil several different functions. The ideal flyer is postcard- or A5-sized, and it should be glossy. Although actual postcards with the same design on them as the flyer can be useful, they are restrictive in that they can't have extra information printed on them in the future. The front of the flyer should have the band's logo at the top, the picture in the middle, and a wide enough border at the bottom to accommodate further information. In this way the flyers can be used time and time again, and different details can be printed in the bottom border of each edition with a domestic printer – details of a forthcoming gig, for example, for which the flyer guarantees entry, or details of your first release. A brief biography should be printed on the reverse, together with the band's web site address. Below this should be a separate section in which fans can fill in their names, addresses, email addresses and/or phone numbers. This section can be either clipped off and handed in at gigs, or it could be posted to the main band address, which should also be printed on this bottom section.

This section should be headed with something like "Join our FREE INFO SERVICE and we'll mail you details of forthcoming gigs, releases, merchandise and competitions. Fill in your details and post it to us, or hand this flyer in to the band." The purpose of this is to build up a mailing list and database of supporters as quickly as possible. If you want to get more elaborate, you can ask your fans for other details, such as their age (which could be useful if this restricts them from attending certain gigs), other favourite bands (interesting), and which local and national papers they read (useful for targeting advertising and press releases). You could even issue 'membership cards' for the band's information service, and strike deals with local promoters so that they offer reduced admission prices to your gigs to anyone carrying a membership card.

It's important to administer your mailing list properly and keep your fans up to date with your activities, in order to make them feel that they are privy to the inside scoop on the band. This is obviously a lot less expensive if it can be done by email, and also a lot more immediate. You should issue regular newsletters, as well as short bulletins about forthcoming gigs, whilst also ensuring that you save time and money by regularly removing people from the list who seem to have moved or lost interest in the band.

posters

Posters are a bit of a luxury for any band, but they are an effective way of communicating with a local audience. The design of the poster should match that of the front of the flyers described above: logo at the top, picture in the middle, and the bottom quarter of the poster left blank for further information. The band's website address should also feature prominently. Although you're unlikely to be able to use a domestic printer to add information onto the posters – which should be at least A3 size – you should be able to make this work with a bit of judicious photocopying and plenty of glue, unless you can afford to invest in new print runs each time.

Flyposting is illegal in many areas, and even where it's acceptable the main sites are often controlled by different flyposting firms that will take a dim views of you encroaching onto their sites. You can still get good coverage by talking the local venues, pubs, cafes, shops and local colleges into displaying your posters; it will simply take some front and a bit of footwork. Your efforts should prove worthwhile, however – people notice posters, and if they see yours they will be impressed that here is a band that is together and going places. Local promoters, in particular, have much more respect for bands that they can see are putting a real effort into making everyone aware of them.

Depending on the design of your poster, as well as on the kind of music you play, posters have a surprising amount of appeal as a merchandise item. Even if you're selling them for £1 or £2, if you sell enough then in the long run it could cover the costs of the posters you've had to use for promotion.

printing

These days you're not stuck with the option of either having your material produced by local printers, who may be few and far between, or regular high street print shops, which tend to be expensive; with email, design for posters and leaflets can be sent almost anywhere, and you make make considerable savings this way, even when taking into account the courier charges involved in having the finished posters and flyers sent to you. One of the best places to start looking for deals on posters and flyers on a national level is in *Exchange & Mart*.

checklist

To finish, then, you should sort out the following areas before you can move ahead:

- Band partnership and songwriting split agreements

- Song copyrights protected

- Band solicitor and accountant

- Band account and delegated finance person

- Band name agreed and protected, and band logo

- Band headed paper, phone and fax numbers, and email address

- 'Label' headed paper

- Band biography, photograph(s), flyers and posters

- Delegated person in charge of communication

It's no easy task getting all of the above elements in order, and the way you approach them will say a great deal about your overall approach to your career. It's possible to sort out some or all of them as you go along, but I would suggest that if you can deal with most of them at the beginning then your stronger will be built on a stronger foundation.

Now all that remains is the minor issue of making some brilliant recordings, releasing them, and making some money. Read on.

recording

Now that you're brimming with motivation, and have set up the band to operate as a stand-alone entity, we can move on to the sharp end of the business. For the purposes of this chapter, we will assume that the band has some limited studio experience but has never recorded with the intention of commercially releasing the finished product.

Recording for commercial release has an entirely different set of parameters than recording a series of demos. If you've been making demos for the purpose of attracting the attention of record companies then you've probably been working from the perspective of recording adequate and representative versions of your songs, rather than creating proper masters. At this point, however, you'll be creating recordings that will have to stand up to critical scrutiny from not just the press, and possibly radio, but also the audience, whom you'll be asking to part with their hard-earned cash.

existing recordings

Most bands who have been together for a certain amount of time will have done some kind of recording, to varying degrees of technical quality. Perhaps some four-track demos have been circulated, or – if the band gigs regularly – there may be a live tape either sold at gigs or used to promote the band. If you've been together for a while, you may have a rag-bag collection of various recordings, some of which may feature former members of the band.

Although money is inevitably going to be pretty tight, it's counter-productive to release existing material that has already done the rounds. For a start, most of those people who follow the band's progress will have already heard it, and therefore so might some of the local press, and the fact that it's been re-submitted to them on a nice shiny CD with a proper inlay card isn't going to make them change their views of the material itself. There will be no sense of excitement about the material, and a potential selling point will have been lost. Remember also that, as you're making recordings to sell this time, they are more likely to achieve this goal if they are brand new.

At this point, the sensible thing to do, creatively, is to decide to start from scratch, and resolve to record new material which captures the band's performances and songwriting as they are now, rather than as they were then. If you write down a list of every song that the band currently has in its repertoire you'll soon be able to identify which are the strongest songs in a live situation, and which are the strongest songs overall. Assuming that you've been gigging regularly, playing both headline and support sets, then it's not unreasonable to assume that you might have, say, 15 songs or so that pass muster, and perhaps some older tracks that you occasionally play live.

Whilst considering this list, it's only natural that, if there are several writers in the band, each will want their songs to be top of the list for a new recording session; however, it's important to pick those songs which have the most chance of achieving the goals of the release. For example, it may be agreed that a particular song has the best chance of getting onto the radio, despite the fact that you don't think that it's the best song in itself, or that you're bored with it.

formats

The first thing that needs to be decided is how many tracks to record, as this will dictate the format of the eventual release. Of course, the format will be determine to a large extent by budget, but there are other factors that need to be taken into account before any decision is made concerning recording. What follows is a list of possible formats to consider, along with the advantages and disadvantages of each.

singles

Advantages

Singles (two or three tracks) are cheap to record and master, and under most package deals the manufacturing costs are lower than albums. Artwork also tends to be less elaborate, and thus cheaper to reproduce. Singles are a great calling card for a band, and provide new listeners with a snapshot of how they sound. The single is also the standard review format in many national and local music publications or columns, and in terms of radio play the single is practically the only game in town.

Disdavantages

The sale of singles has a very small profit margin, even assuming that distributors can sell them to dealers at full price. They seem to be good value at 99 pence a shot, but not such good value at £3.99. *Pro rata*, their recording, mastering and manufacturing costs don't reduce to one sixth of a twelve-track album. They are perceived as disposable items, with a short lifespan. As well as this, the fact that a single is meant to be a snapshot of a band's best work can backfire if people in the media don't like it.

Recording a single should therefore be undertaken from the perspective of achieving some press reviews and perhaps some radio play, stimulating general interest in the band and hopefully generating enough sales income to cover its costs. There is no doubt that people still regard the single very much as one lead A-side track and then a B-side, which is perceived as less important. On the radio, certainly, the focus will be entirely on the lead track, and this is also true of any press reviews.

The decision to record a single must therefore be based on the examination of special production criteria, which we will examine later.

EPs

Advantages

EPs ('Extended Play'), complete with a lead track and then two or three other tracks, are a good way of introducing the audience and the press to a band. For a start, they are perceived as a credible format. EPs are still relatively cheap to record and master, and can be manufactured at the same cost as singles. Also, if one track is nominated as the lead track, they may be plugged for radio play. For the eventual purchaser, EPs are better value than singles, and they are just as likely to be reviewed in the press.

Disadvantages

EPs can still only be sold for a relatively low price, although this is likely to be higher than a single, or at least not as discounted. There may also be problems with achieving radio play. EPs can still be perceived as disposable items, much the same as singles.

An EP is therefore a good introduction to a band, and may still achieve some radio play on the lead track, which has implications not only for the production but also for the choice of lead track. Many highly-regarded bands have made their mark with a series of EPs, some tracks of which are later compiled to form an album or mini album.

mini albums

Advantages

Although recording and releasing a mini album is significantly more expensive than it is for a single, they can be sold at a much higher margin. Mini albums – which traditionally include between five and seven tracks – are an accepted format, particularly as a first release for an indie band, and can provide an excellent introduction to a band. They are also almost as likely to be reviewed in the albums sections of the monthly and weekly music papers and magazines as a full-length album.

Disadvantages

The cost of recording and mastering up to seven tracks may not be significantly less than a full album. Similarly, the artwork required for a mini album will be just as elaborate as that required for a full-length album, and this will also be true of the manufacturing costs (which may involve, for example, a full jewel case). However, the sale price of a mini album will inevitably be substantially lower than that of a full-length album. Not only that, but radio play is much less likely than it is for a single or an EP.

As with EPs, many bands have launched their careers with one or more well-received mini albums, perhaps on independent labels, before being signed. A mini album is fairly easily digestible material for a press reviewer, although with no lead track it's unlikely to be played on the radio, except maybe on specialist shows or if a producer or DJ is hugely impressed with the band.

albums

Advantages

Albums have more than seven tracks, or are over 35 minutes in running time, and are seen as the most credible and significant format that a band can release. The album format is also that which is sold at the highest price and profit margin. They are perceived as long-term projects that define a band's sound at a certain point in time, and are most likely to catch the attention of distributors. They also lend themselves well to press reviews in both the weekly and monthly music press.

Disadvantages

Clearly, the recording and mastering costs of a full album are going to be the most expensive of all of the formats available to the aspiring band. Because it's necessary for albums to be sold at a relatively high price in order that they maintain their perceived value, this may put off the casual purchaser. In terms of press coverage, albums are seen as a definite statement of a band's music, unlike singles and EPs, which are seen to be short-term formats. If the reviews are unfavourable, the entire perception of the band may be threatened, at least in the short term. Also, radio play will be confined to specialist shows.

Making an album is thus a relatively portentous step for a new band, even assuming that the material is of such high quality that a whole album can be sustained. There is little point in recording an album for its own sake, which may end up having some strong tracks which are then let down by a series of filler tracks. The money could be better spent elsewhere.

the ideal format

It's impossible to suggest an ideal format that will fit every artist's requirements. In terms of alternative or indie artists (much as we all dislike musical labels!), I would suggest the release of either a single or a mini album. If budget is an issue (and it always is), a fantastic two- or three-track single will certainly advance the band's career, and the resulting sales may in time recover its costs. If funds permit, a mini album will provide a great introduction to the band without carrying the weight and significance of a full album release.

If there is adequate budget and a huge amount of very strong material, making an album will undoubtedly raise the possibility of generating the greatest cash return, and will also create a long-term product that the band can promote for a considerable length of time.

recording

Once the songs to be recorded have been established, a budget for the recording session should be worked out as accurately as possible. The first factor to be considered is the choice of studio.

studios and engineers

You should already be familiar with all of the studios in your immediate area, although it's a good idea to refresh your information about them on a regular basis in case their equipment has been upgraded, their rates have changed, or the in-house staff have moved on. If possible, you should aim to complete recording in one session, with a break between recording and mixing. Every artist records in a different way, but as a general rule it would be unusual if less than a day was spent on recording each track, and about the same amount of time on each mix. Some time may be saved during the mixing process if there are some tracks that have similar requirements.

You should try and resist the temptation to simply record at the same studio at which you've recorded material in the past, and you should also make a full assessment of all of the studios which are available to you. It may be the case that you can obtain a more professional-sounding result by spending more time in a basic studio than less time in an expensive one. Assuming that you don't want (or can't afford) to bring in a separate producer, one of the deciding factors will be the in-house engineer. If you have demos of the songs you want to have recorded, it's important to take the time to meet with the engineer well in advance of the session in order to discuss ideas about how you want the finished tracks to sound. You should bring along some albums by other artists which you feel sound similar to the sound you want, and then discuss how you can best achieve this. (The engineer may suggest using a different drum kit, for example, or think you should try experimenting with different combinations of guitars and amps.)

This kind of discussion will often prove to be particularly useful, and may even end up leading you to reconsider some key decisions. A passing comment from the engineer may inspire you to look at a song in a completely different way – if he or she suggests listening to another artist's album and then imagining how your track would sound if you used some of the same ideas, for example. In this case, it's important to be as open-minded as possible – this may be the first time that a professional has listened to your music in detail, and their comments may be surprising and challenging.

There's no point turning up for an expensive recording session with the intention of making recordings ready for release if this is your first encounter with the engineer. You'll achieve better results if the two of you can establish a rapport before the session.

studios

Every studio is different, and you'll need to make sure that the one you've chosen is the right one before committing yourselves to a session there. Certain factors will be obvious, of course; for example, if the members of the rhythm section need to play together and still be able to see each other, will the studio's live room and isolation booths allow this? If the drummer has a larger than average kit, will it all fit in the live room? How many headphone mixes are available, and how many do you need? If possible, you should listen to as much material from other bands that has recently been recorded in the same studio as possible.

The studio may have an old desk, which may sound fantastic, but if it's equipped with inadequate outboard gear the final mixes will inevitably not be as good as they could. You should check that the studio has a wide selection of microphones, at least a few options in guitar and bass amps, and keyboards. You will also need to consider more aesthetic features: for example, is the control room incredibly cramped? If it is, it will be difficult to concentrate on playing if the whole band want to be in there.

Very good results can be obtained in good 16-track studios and basic 24-track facilities. Depending on the type of band, an eight-track studio is probably not enough (unless, for example, you are a solo singer/songwriter, duo or in a primarily acoustic band), and a 48-track studio is almost certainly over the top.

studio deals

Most mid-range and low-budget studios will contemplate negotiating a deal with you (unless they happened to be incredibly busy and are in the position of being able to turn away work), especially if cash is involved. It's important to make sure that you pin down the following details before striking any deal with a studio:

- How many hours does the 'daily rate' cover (ten hours would be usual) and what is the hourly rate for every extra hour worked?

- Does the studio rate cover the hiring of the engineer and all of his or her expenses, or are there extras involved, such as having to pay his or her cab fare home after a certain time of night?

- What does the studio charge for extras, such as instrument hire (and is this hourly or daily?), and items such as multitrack tape, analogue cassettes and DAT cassettes?

- If the studio is going to add a mark-up value to the price of the tape it buys from wholesalers, would it therefore be cheaper to bring your own tapes?

- Is there any catering at the studio of any description? If not, where is the nearest café or pub?

- Do all of the studio costs have VAT added to them, or are they VAT inclusive?

Once you've managed to iron out all of these points, calculate how much money you have available and then ask the studio if they are prepared to accept a reduced deal for cash on the day. If you're lucky, they may also include instrument hire. At the end of the day they can only say no, and even if you save yourself £50 it's well worth doing.

It is not necessarily a good idea to go for an all-inclusive deal, an overnight deal or a 'lockout' arrangement, unless this suits your schedule, and you're confident that you (and the engineer) have the stamina.

On rare occasions, studios may be prepared to work for reduced rates, on the basis that in turn they receive a share of the income obtained from sales of the finished product – a so-called 'points deal'. (A 'point' is industry slang for a royalty percentage point, by which 'three points' means 3%.) Anything that may reduce the initial overhead is worth looking into, unless you feel that the studio or engineer are angling to obtain some kind of ongoing ownership of the rights in the finished recordings. If you receive such an offer, discuss it with your lawyer, while at the same time bearing in mind that the legal costs you incur in arriving at a deal with the studio may outweigh any savings you make.

Once you've struck up a deal with the studio, the sensible thing to do is to ask them for a quote in writing, under the proviso that there will be no extra costs imposed above this quote, unless they are specifically agreed by the band during the session. In this way, if the engineer begins using some piece of equipment that is charged at a higher rate, you can then dispute the cost if you were unaware that it was being used.

Beware of hidden charges, and beware also of VAT. If the quote from the studio has terms and conditions attached to it in small print, be sure to read them carefully.

credits

Credits are another grey area, and it's best to be clear about them well before any recordings are made. We have assumed that the band is effectively producing the session itself, using the engineer purely as that: an engineer. In other words, the band will be calling the shots during the session and, although they will undoubtedly consider the engineer's advice carefully, the final decisions will rest with them. However, the engineer may wish to co-produce the session with the band if he or she feels that they can provide a significant level of creative input. If the engineer makes this offer purely in order that they are then entitled to receive a co-producer's credit on the finished product, it's a simple decision for the band whether or not they wish to involve him or her in this way; however, if the band suspect that the offer to co-produce – or even produce – their material is merely a pretext under which to demand a separate fee, or indeed some royalty points, then this should be resisted.

booking the session

You should discuss the recording schedule with the studio well in advance, and you should plan to have a gap between the completion of recording and the mixing session of perhaps as much as a week. Aim to reach the end of the recording session with rough monitor mixes of each track so that each member of the band can take them away and take some time to consider what might be the right approach to mixing the material.

pre-production

Recording in the studio is much like decorating: it's all in the preparation. Ideally, the band should perform as many gigs as possible before committing themselves to a recording session, as this is guaranteed to tighten up the songs which are to be recorded. If this cannot be arranged, however, a considerable amount of rehearsing will be necessary to ensure that the band is well prepared before undertaking any studio work. During the rehearsing process, songs can be tried out in a number of different ways, mistakes can be ironed out, and any misunderstandings about what everyone is meant to be playing can be laid to rest.

Always take a tape recorder into rehearsals with you, and record as you go along, making sure that everyone listens to the tapes at the next session. If any songs involve vocal harmonies, these will need to be practiced rigorously *a capella* so that everyone understands their parts. There are few things more frustrating that wasting money in booking the studio, only to find that you still have to sort out harmonies that should have been learned and perfected during rehearsals.

You should also try experimenting with different guitar sounds, and the more effects you can lay your hands on the better. If you have a choice of amplifiers, it's best to assume that in the studio you're going to be needing them. Try to avoid the temptation to simply use your existing live sounds, and try more adventurous variations.

If at all possible, the engineer who will be working with you in the studio should come down to final rehearsals, if they are taking more than a passing interest in the band. (And if not, why are you working with them?) Play through all the songs, and listen to their comments and suggestions in order to perform any final fine-tuning and arranging.

Once the songs have been sorted out in terms of their arrangements and the way they feel (bearing in mind that some of them may have been replaced at this stage by other songs which the band now feel would be better to record), it's possible to turn your attention to more practical matters. Try to head off any problems that you may experience with your instruments in the studio by making sure that your guitars are set up properly and don't buzz, that all of your amps are all working and sound clean, and that the drums are properly tuned. You should also make sure that there are plenty of spare strings for guitars and basses, and also spare drum heads. For vocalists, it's unwise to be singing constantly during rehearsals right up to the day before the recording session, and as the end of rehearsals approaches you should back off on vocals as much as you can.

Before starting work in the studio, you should already have worked out your ideal schedule which sets out what you hope to have attained at the end of each day. It would also be beneficial to discuss the schedule with the engineer before starting work, in case he feels that it's too ambitious.

the recording session

You should arrive early on the first day, making sure that you get on with setting up the drums first whilst the rest of the band check their instruments. Once everything is set up, allow the engineer to mic things up the way he or she wants, as this will save significant amounts of time. After all, the engineer works in the studio regularly and knows its idiosyncrasies and what will get the best results. In the same way that it's *always* a good idea to buy a sound engineer a drink at a gig, it's also well worth finding out how the engineer likes his or her tea, and to keep a constant supply going.

Engineers are normally a shy and retiring species, and masters of diplomacy. If you ask them which of two ideas sounds better they may well plump for the one which gets them home earlier (unless they have a keen interest in the band). If you're happy then usually they're happy as well, and it can sometimes be a lot of work to coax them off the fence. The more open your relationship with him or her, however, the more opinions will be forthcoming, and very often the end result will show a significant improvement.

Assuming that you're on schedule, try to lay down some guide vocals very early on, as you may be surprised at how often these end up being used in a final mix. Concentrate on feel and performance rather than spending too much time on perfecting individual sounds (many of which can be radically altered in the mix, in any case). Also, make sure that all instruments are in tune (preferably all to the same tuner). Guitars can often be recorded dry, without reverb, which can then be applied during the mixing process. This will prevent a good take from being ruined by the fact it sounds like it's been recorded under water.

Although it's difficult to generalise, in terms of instrumentation and arrangements it's better to err on the side of simplicity and space rather than to load each track with everything, including the kitchen sink. One subtle killer guitar riff is worth a dozen huge tom fills and massive vocal harmonies. If you're going to go for the kitchen sink approach, however, it's often better to include additional material and effects bit by bit, so that these elements are introduced to the listener gradually over the course of the song. If you use samplers or decks, it's also worth finding out all about the copyright implications of this.

If one particular track doesn't seem to be gelling together, take a short break and move on to something else. If you try to make running repairs, this will affect the entire schedule, and you may be left with finished versions of all of the tracks which have been rushed. You should never, under any circumstances, rush vocals or try to cram them all in on one take.

It's only natural for you to have high hopes for one or two particular tracks from the session, and if these are those with which you encounter problems it may be simply the pressure of meeting your own expectations that is causing the problem. It's a much better idea to take a break, move onto another track, and come back to that track the following day.

Too many artists – particularly those who are inexperienced in the studio –

make the mistake of not commenting on things about which they are unhappy, and letting them pass. It's always best to speak up if you think something sounds strange, or if a vocal is flat, even if you can't clearly express exactly what you think is wrong. It's much better to deal with such problems at the time than to try and go back and sort them out later, when time is even tighter. Be wary if anyone says anything like "we'll sort it out in the mix", as that tends to translate as "we won't be able to sort it out in the mix"!

If you find that you're falling behind schedule, perhaps having to lay down the rhythm tracks for all of the songs you're recording at once, you'll have to make the decision to either reduce the number of tracks you want to have at the end of the session or, if you can afford it, book more studio time. However, remember that, if you end up buying the multitrack tape and taking it away with you at the end of the session, you can always return to finish off the tracks you have set aside when funds permit. The last thing you need at this point is to suffer from any more pressure than you're already experiencing.

Inexperienced bands often forget that the vocals are more important than *any* other instrument. No one cares that the snare drum fill into the second chorus is fantastic if the singer is flat. It's the first thing that imprints itself on the listeners (especially the A&R people). A lot of great live singers get a shock in the studio at how spot on their pitching has to be. The engineer will often record four or five takes and then make a composite ('comp') vocal using the best bits from each take rather than hope for one killer take.

It's worth working out how many tracks are used up by your most complex song, as this technique eats up the available tracks. A lot of vocalists can find the whole studio experience daunting, but you should still be honest if you think that the vocals aren't in tune, even though this approach runs the risk of destroying the singer's fragile ego.

As far as drums are concerned, it may be worth experimenting with a click track (assuming that your drummer doesn't already play to one). This has the advantage of keeping the track in time, which helps everyone else to record their parts. It also means that the keyboards could be recorded via MIDI, which frees up audio tracks as well as allowing a choice of keyboard sounds, at least until the final mix, if the studio has a sequencer running in sync with the audio. It's also possible (especially in digital studios) to drop in on drum tracks, or even to comp them. Even if you decide not to use a click track, it's well worth working out the tempo of each song at the pre-production stage. Sometimes even a difference of a couple of beats per minute can drastically change the feel of a song.

As the end of the session nears, you need to be moving onto rough mixes or 'monitor mixes', which can be dumped down onto cassette so that each member of the band can take them away and listen to them.

mixing

As stated previously, it's enormously beneficial to make sure that you take a break of even a few days between recording and mixing in order to give everyone a chance to get used to the rough mixes. If possible, you should also take the multitrack tape of the sessions away from the studio with you and store it somewhere safe. (This isn't meant to imply that you shouldn't trust studios, but mistakes have been known to happen.)

During the mixing process, it's best to allow the engineer to get a rough mix up on the desk before everyone starts chiming in with their opinions. It's only natural for everyone to want their particular parts to be the loudest of all, but an experienced engineer will be aware of this and compensate for it in a way which should please everyone.

Once a final mix is within sight, you should listen to it on a few different sets of speakers before agreeing that it's of sufficiently high quality, and if you have enough time then a couple of different versions should be put down with the lead vocal at different levels. On singles, or on EPs which have a lead track, there should also be at least one mix which has the lead vocal removed – a so called 'TV track' – which can then be used if the band are called upon to mime the song on television with a live lead vocal. Well, you never know.

Similarly, with singles and EPs, you will need to mix a track with an view to how it's going to sound on the radio. This may call for extra compression, or an edit to reduce the track's length.

After a safety copy has been taken, the final mixes should then be put down onto DAT or CD-R, and enough cassettes should be run off for each of the band members.

I can't state strongly enough that there should be plenty of time spent on making sure that the vocals and the mix sound right. It's worth taking breaks so that you can compare the mix with CDs of other bands which have a similar sound to that which you're trying to capture. The mixing process can often carry on late into the night, and it's often worth getting a mix up, sleeping on it, and then listening with fresh ears in the morning before committing it to history.

Recording on a tight budget is nerve-wracking exercise. There's never enough time to arrive at something with which everyone's happy, and it's not easy for every band member to have the spotlight turned on them as another tenner ticks away. It's vital to keep calm and try and think of the big picture. It's also worth remembering that perfection doesn't guarantee a hit; sometimes it's the sloppiness and mistakes that lend a song and a band character and warmth.

mastering, artwork and manufacturing

Now that you've left the studio with the tracks for a blockbuster album or single on either DAT or CD-R, it's time need to make some important decisions on how best to proceed and release your record. The next stages in the creation of a completed record are mastering, artwork and manufacturing, and these are all areas in which, with a bit of forward planning, you can save some money while maintaining the quality of your product.

Your ultimate goal is the release of product which not only sounds as professional as possible, and justifies the amount of time, money and effort which you've invested in the recording process, but is also released with a memorable title and striking artwork.

mastering

Before you can proceed much further, your recordings will need to be mastered. During the mastering process, you can either significantly alter the sound of your finished studio recordings or you can leave them exactly as they are – assuming, or course, that you're totally happy with the way they sound through the speakers in the mastering studio.

Although it's easy to change the proposed running order of the tracks during mastering, it will save time if you experiment with configuring the tracks in different combinations while you're at at home, either on cassette or by using the CD-R (which you will have taken out of the studio). The mastering engineer may well make suggestions on the running order that work better than yours, as he or she will be attuned to some problems of which you may be unaware (ie there may be too many songs in a row in the same key, or at the same tempo, or there may be some odd-sounding fades).

Mastering in sophisticated studios using multiband digital techniques is now relatively cheap, costing anywhere from between £50 and £100 per hour, depending on the deals offered by the studio. As most professional mastering facilities use similar equipment, the most crucial element in mastering is the quality and personality of the engineer.

During the mastering process, the general clarity and definition of your recordings can be improved. Unwanted hiss and hum can be removed, dropouts can be corrected, and sections of tracks or even individual words can be edited. EQ can also be added, to give spread and depth to the finished track. To a limited extent, tracks can be sped up or slowed down to the point at which the lead vocal starts to sound unusual.

You should certainly be prepared to meet up with a mastering engineer before a session, if they have time, both to examine the facilities at your disposal and also to discuss what you're looking for in the finished master. You could play him a few tracks by other bands that you think sound close to what you want, and the engineer will be able to suggest approaches that might be taken to emulate that type of sound.

There is no hard-and-fast rule about the amount of time a mastering session will take; a two-track single might well only take an hour, although this doesn't necessarily mean that a twelve-track album will take six hours. It may be wise to consider mastering an album in two sessions, as your critical faculties will become dull after a few hours in the studio.

You'll need to discuss the fades on certain tracks and the gaps between individual tracks exhaustively during the session, until you eventually arrive at a finished master. This can then be dumped down onto a CD-R or DAT. You should also take a safety copy of your final master.

Mastering facilities often have deals running for the manufacture of final CDs and also CD-Rs. You should order a reasonable number of CD-R samples of your finished master, and it may make financial sense to order these from the same facility as that at which you carried out the mastering. Even if this works out as being slightly more expensive than you could find elsewhere, remember that it would cost you money to courier or post the master to another facility, and at this point in the proceedings time is often of the essence.

CD-Rs with printed inlay cards and on-body printing should cost between £1.75 and £3 each, depending on the quantity you order and how complicated the accompanying artwork. There are a number of reasons for manufacturing CD-R samples, including the following:

- To generate interest among distributors and potential licensees in advance of the manufacture of your finished product

- To allow the possibility of radio play, if the opportunity arises before your product has been manufactured

- To enable you to send out advance review copies to any publications which will publish their review in conjunction with the release of your product

The CD-R should therefore have the following information contained on the inlay card. (Again, the fictional band Sanctuary are used as an example.)

SANCTUARY

Advance album: *Quasimodo's Revenge*

[Track listing – titles and times]

Produced by Neil Gotrich

XYZ Records [logo and contact details]

All songs written by Rimadonna/Paul. © 2000. Copyright control.

© 2000. The copyright in these sound recordings is owned by XYZ Records. All rights reserved.

The only thing missing is the catalogue number, which you will have to decide with your distributor(s), as each will have different requirements concerning the numbering and lettering of catalogue numbers.

artwork

The more elaborate your artwork then the more it will cost, both to produce and to print. However, there is no point in doing it on the cheap and ending up with an amateur-looking record, and you must strike a balance between creating a memorable and intriguing cover for your release and working within the budget you have available.

It's impossible to generalise about artwork, but the current trend in the genres of indie and dance (those labels again!) is to avoid using a shot of the artist on the cover of the release and instead to use some connected image which is simple and striking. This trend is currently spreading to other musical genres.

By this stage you should have a good band logo, and it would be strange not to use it on your album and single sleeve, unless you use a new logo which is then used on all future correspondence, posters and flyers. On no account should you change the band logo just after your first release, as this will make the release seem out of date almost immediately.

The technical requirements necessary for the production of artwork will vary significantly, depending on the manufacturer you choose to use and, of course, on the format(s) you choose to release. If you're working with an experienced graphic designer or artist it should be fairly straightforward, as most of the larger manufacturers issue details of their technical requirements on their web sites. However, problems can arise if you use a designer who has only limited expertise in the specialist practise of producing artwork for CDs, cassettes and vinyl; it's expensive to correct mistakes or reprint material, so be sure that you're absolutely confident in the abilities of the person you're hiring.

It's vital that any image you use on the artwork is free of any copyright problems – in other words, you should either own it or reach an agreement with the copyright owner or photographer (who are often the same person) that you may use the image, free of charge or for a fee. Don't under any circumstances use any photograph or other image which you're uncertain that you're allowed to use legally – remanufacturing is an expensive process.

You should also be as creative as your budget will allow with the artwork on the body of the CD itself, perhaps using one striking colour with the band's logo on the silver surface of the CD. On almost all commercially-released CDs, it's traditional to have the relevant copyright information printed on the outer edge of the disc itself, as well as on the inlay card. Also, most commercially-released CDs include a barcode, although this is an expense that you can avoid if you're unsuccessful in landing a traditional distribution deal for your product. If a barcode is required after the finished product has been manufactured, a barcode sticker can be used.

You may decide against including the lyrics on the inlay card – they may look strange when written out, or it may prove to be a prohibitively expensive and time-consuming process to reproduce them. In accordance with the current absence of artist's pictures on CD front covers, the current trend is that less is more, and in many cases this extends to omitting the lyrics to a release.

You should obtain colour proofs of your artwork for approval, which will save enormous disappointment if the final colours don't match or the design isn't what you had in mind. If everything is okay, you can now proceed to manufacture your product.

manufacturing

You should almost always choose to release your product on CD, and the good news is that CD manufacturing has probably never been cheaper. Even so, genres such as indie and dance still have a significant market for vinyl releases, and it would be almost unimaginable for a dance track not to be released on a 12" single, however small the manufactured quantity.

Many small indie labels release limited runs of singles on CD, along with a smaller number on coloured vinyl. They do this in order to turn the vinyl version into an exclusive collectors item, stimulating interest in the release as a whole. This is not a cheap endeavour, however, and it may not be cost-effective to manufacture only 500 vinyl singles, as the cost of doing so may incur a deficit for the entire release, even if you sell every CD and vinyl copy.

Manufacturers often have a number of deals available on quantities of CDs as low as 300. However, if you're working with a distributor you'll need to determine exactly many copies the distributor is likely to want in stock as of the day of release, how many you intend to use for marketing and promotional purposes, and how many you'll need to sell at gigs in the immediate future. For this reason, it's hard to imagine that you would need fewer than 1,000 copies of an album or single release to achieve your goals.

It's very important that you shop around for deals, among both manufacturers and mastering suites. However, it's of paramount importance to examine exactly what is included in each quote, right down to determining whether or not delivery is included. For example, if you're in a band from Scotland and you use a London-based manufacturer who gives you the best per-copy deal, you're going to find that shipping 1,000 units to Scotland is going to be expensive, and that shipping 500 copies to Scotland and 500 to your distributor is going to cost even more.

Remember that you own the manufactured stock, and that, if you run out, you can always acquire more from that which is being held by your distributor. You should also be aware of the turnaround time which your manufacturer will need, if you're in the happy situation that you've sold out and you need to manufacture new stock.

publishing

Although an exhaustive explanation of music publishing is outside the scope of this book, you must be aware that you will have to make payments to the MCPS for product that you sell. This means that you will have to contact the MCPS and obtain a mechanical licence, and then make payments at the statutory mechanical rate when you manufacture. The MCPS will then pass on your payments to their appropriate members, including music publishers and those songwriters whose songs you may have covered on your record.

Until this point, however, we have assumed that your band are recording and releasing their own material (in other words, your songs are written by all or some of the band). Even so, it's still a wise move to go through the process of registering your songs with the PRS and the MCPS and meeting the actual payments which songwriters are due. We aren't talking about huge sums of money being involved here (if we're assuming limited quantities of sales), and the songwriters may elect to pass these funds back into the band on a temporary basis. However, if the band splits up, or members leave after the release of commercial product (or at least that product sold at gigs), then in terms of publishing it's important that your house is in order right from the beginning.

chapter 5

releasing your product

Anyone with a bit of money can make a record. Hopefully, you will have made – or are about to make – a great record. This could take the form of a superb single that will make people wake up and take notice of the band, or a fantastic debut album that will stand the test of time. However, none of this matters if, at the end of the day, your current audience and also your potential audience are not made aware of the record, or – even if they are aware of it – are not able to buy it.

The next few chapters will look into the nuts and bolts of how a product is released, marketed and sold. Now that the creative work on the record has ended, you will need to alter the way in which you perceive the work you have created. At this point, you will have completed material, either on DAT or CD-R, which you must be prepared to release, warts and all. At this stage, there is little point in dwelling on aspects of the creative work on the record, worrying that perhaps it could have been done better, and it's too late to be worrying about the mix, the running order, the artwork or the title.

You will now need to concentrate on one thing alone: making as many people aware of your product as possible, and selling as many copies of it as you can. Some readers may be twitching slightly at the use of the expression 'product', but that's exactly what we're dealing with here. Your 'art', for want of a better word, is the material on the record and on the artwork. From now on, you'll be dealing with the product – the stuff that comes in boxes – and working out how best to get it out there.

distribution

'Distribution' is a term used in the music industry to describe the various methods used by record companies to get their product sold and then delivered into the hands of dealers, who can then sell the product to the public. Distribution companies are either completely independent or, in some cases, partially or fully controlled by the major record companies or their parent companies. However, this doesn't mean that the distribution departments of major record companies deal only with the product released by their label; they'll also act as the distributor for any number of other labels with whom they have a distribution arrangement.

The distribution arrangements employed by record companies can be enormously different. A small distributor may keep its stock in the warehouse of a much larger distributor, receive sales orders and then instruct its larger partner to physically deliver the product, splitting the distribution commission between them. Distributors make their money by exacting a percentage of the price at which they sell their finished product, and passing the remainder back to their clients (usually record companies).

Some distributors have huge telesales departments, through which dealers can phone in their orders, as well as an on-line ordering system and a fleet of reps on the road whose job it is to maintain contacts with dealers, inform them of forthcoming releases and to make sure that their shelves are fully stocked. These teams are sometimes called as 'strike forces', and they work on what are termed 'priority' records, ensuring that stock levels are maintained and certain 'offers' are made to dealers, to help ensure a healthy chart position for the product in question. These offers can include giving the dealers free stock, discounts, or even multiple deals, whereby the dealers can obtain three records for the price of two, for example. What follows is a list of the options available to you to get your product sold and distributed.

scheduling

The first point to make is that, for a number of reasons, you will need to make all of your decisions about distribution well before the time of manufacturing. If you can persuade a distributor to handle your product, or if you can strike a deal with a small label on a licensing basis (a subject covered in detail in chapter ten, 'Licensing'), then this may well have a bearing on the number of units you decide to manufacture, and will also affect other practical points, such as where your manufactured stock ends up being stored. Similarly, you may be able to take advantage of the manufacturing arrangements of the distributor or label and get a better deal for your stock. In certain circumstances, you may also be able to obtain an advance from the distributor, set against your share of the sales income. Also, your choice of distribution arrangements may also affect your choice of catalogue number.

Finally, the distributor may hold strong views about your proposed release date, and will want to ensure that your release achieves maximum sales.

As soon as your product is recorded and mastered, you should have manufactured some advance tapes or CD-Rs, as discussed in the previous chapter. Assuming that your band has begun to attract some attention in the local and perhaps national press, and has a following which is starting to grow outside your local area, then there's no reason why a distributor (perhaps not a major distributor, but a distributor nonetheless) wouldn't consider handling your product.

finding a distributor

This is much easier if your music already falls within a specific genre. Your research to date should have furnished you with a comprehensive list of bands and labels operating in the same musical 'pond' as yourself. (Remember: at this point you should be thinking of yourself as a label). You will probably be a regular reader of *Music Week* by now, and so it should be an easy task to discover the distributors used by the various labels and find one that seems to cover your style of music. Call them up initially to find out who at the distribution company deals with that particular label, or even call the label themselves. Most distribution companies have several 'label managers', whose job it is to liaise with their clients (the labels), in order to make sure that the various products pass smoothly through their system and to put together successful release strategies.

It may not be easy to track down the right person to talk to on the phone, but you may provoke a response if you send a letter or fax and attach some reviews and a biography to this, along with your completed CD-R or cassette. Alternatively, you could try sending an e-mail to the person in question, including a link to the band's web site. Your case will be helped enormously if the label manager at the distribution company really likes your material, rather than simply viewing your approach as nothing more than a business arrangement. Often, the real music enthusiasts in the business are to be found within distribution companies, rather than record companies, perhaps because they deal with a wider range of product and are right up at the sharp end of the market: delivering it to the public.

If a distributor agrees to handle your product, you have taken a huge step forward. Your product will now be available in the shops – or at least in those that order it. You may even have a rack with your name on it at the local HMV. Your next step is to make sure that you maximise on this new situation, and work with the distributor to work out on a sensible and achievable strategy.

release strategy

Whether you're working with a label to whom you've licensed your product or acting as your own label under a direct deal with a distributor, no distributor will be willing to release your product into a vacuum. In other words, there's little point in manufacturing thousands of CDs only to have them sitting expectantly in the distributor's warehouse, waiting for order from dealers – who would have presumably discovered about your product by telepathy.

Your release will need to be properly prepared, which will involve a concentrated effort on marketing and promotion, in conjunction with your distributor. (This subject is covered in detail in the following chapter.) The most important point to consider is that you'll be dealing with a time scale that may perhaps be much longer than you first envisaged, largely because other people are now becoming involved. For example, you may have a complete single or album ready in May, only for the distributor to strongly suggest that you refrain from releasing the finished product until September, for a number of good reasons.

The distributor will also need to discuss the pricing of your product in some detail. Rather than automatically releasing it at a top-line price, they may instead suggest releasing it at a lower price initially to stimulate sales, or even releasing it in limited numbers at a discounted price. At the end of the day, the distributor is in the same business as you, and shares your goal: to sell as many copies of your product as possible, and to generate the largest amount of sales income upon which they can calculate their commission. Accordingly, they are in the best position to provide advice on pricing your product, and you should attempt to resist your natural urge to sell at the highest possible price in order to recoup your investment as quickly as you can. Your aim at this point is to sell the highest number of copies possible (within reason), whatever the price.

All distributors operate to fairly rigid timetables, which work backwards from any proposed release date, taking into accounts such factors as the date when the finished product should turn up at their warehouse, and at which point they will need catalogue numbers for their release schedule. In the weeks leading up to the official release date, the distributor will be pre-selling the release (ie taking orders for it based on the response of dealers to the marketing and promotion that has taken place). The distributor will then arrive at a shipping figure (ie the number of copies delivered to retailers in the first week of release), and will hopefully be taking re-orders as stock sells in the first few weeks.

Distributors have huge amounts of product on their catalogues, and can therefore sometimes be less than pro-active in selling and distributing your product. You shouldn't imagine that the shelves in record stores in every town will be groaning with your album or single – it's up to the individual dealers whether they stock your release or not. Naturally, you will have high hopes for your release, but be prepared for what we should perhaps name the 'Never 'eard Of It' syndrome. This peculiar condition affects all record shop sales staff at some time in their lives, usually when confronted by a member of a band desperately trying to find out whether their record is in stock by pretending to be a fan. Similarly, for a low-key release, there will be only a limited amount of stock available, and this will have to be spread over the entire UK.

If your band is followed by a reasonably large band of supporters, you should be prepared to be bombarded with complaints that they couldn't find your album anywhere. The reasons for this are likely to be numerous, but will probably include the following:

- The dealer they have tried hasn't yet ordered the album, either because they are unaware of its existence, they don't believe that it will sell, or your distributor won't allow them to stock it on a sale-or-return basis

- Your purchaser went into a store which was never likely to take the album in the first place

- It's not out yet. (This happens a lot!)

- The dealer has already had some stock delivered, has sold it all, and is now waiting for a re-order to come in – which is, obviously, the best of all reasons

The only thing to do if your product isn't on the shelves is to make sure that your fans know the catalogue number and distributor of the release, and advise them not to go in to mainstream stores looking for it. Advise them instead that they will be able to pre-order it, buy it or order it from certain independent retailers.

No band or manager likes the thought of disgruntled fans trudging around town being unable to find their record or being told it doesn't exist, but sometimes this is inevitable, considering the sheer volume of product that is released. Problems can be minimised, however, by issuing your fans with the relevant information on how to order your record from certain shops, and striving to work with your distributor in achieving good coverage, in terms of marketing and promotion.

The bible of the music industry is the weekly magazine *Music Week*, to which all dealers subscribe and in which charts illustrating sales are printed. Every week, the magazine prints lists of all of the single and album releases, which are categorised by artist, title, format, catalogue number, label and distributor. Most dealers will keep files of these lists so that they are able answer customer enquiries concerning the release date of a particular record, and your distributor should ensure that *Music Week* is provided with the details of your product well in advance of the release date.

distribution deals

All distributors will require you to sign a distribution deal with them, which will determine the terms upon which they are permitted to sell your product. The main terms of such an agreement will include the commission that the distributor is permitted to deduct from any income generated from product sales (which may be as high as 25%), the term during which they are allowed to sell your product, the discounts they can offer, export rights (whereby they can ship your product to other territories to be sold there), and any other charges they are permitted to deduct (such as stock charges). The distributor is also likely to ask for the right to release your future product.

Although there may be some leeway on the amount of sales commission which distributors can exact when dealing with established artists, deals with new artists are likely to be fairly rigid and non-negotiable. You should use your solicitor to negotiate the agreement, of course, while also taking care not to spend too much on legal costs in attempting to improve those areas of the agreement which are unlikely to be agreed, as it were. You'll need to be realistic, and you should focus your attention on how getting a distributor to work for you will help you financially; in theory, anyone will be able to go into a record shop and order your record, both in the UK and overseas.

It's also worth mentioning that the genre of dance is one where it's infinitely easier to release a limited quantity of 12" singles through a specialist distributor, on the heels of a series of favourable radio reviews and even limited club play. Such releases tend to have an almost guaranteed sales base – of a few hundred copies, at least – largely because any such release is heavily tipped by specialist shops, and will have already sold a a certain number of pre-sales copies.

other methods of distribution

In the event that you can't persuade a distributor to become involved with your product, it's still possible to have it appear in the shops, albeit in a more limited way.

Many small labels effectively operate self-distribution systems (particularly if they deal in a specific genre of music), and sell their product to record shops and wholesalers directly, and to customers by mail order. Although major chains such as HMV and Our Price are fairly rigid in terms of the distributors from whom they receive product, and retailers such as Woolworths stock only a limited range of product, there are huge numbers of independent retailers who will consider taking product directly from a label.

This can be achieved by simply phoning record shops, asking them if they'll stock your produce on a sale-or-return basis, emphasising the amount of marketing and promotion you're undertaking to support with the release, and providing them with any reviews you may have collected. For example, imagine that you're the owner of, or a buyer at, a record shop that specialises exclusively in folk music. There are a number of customers who visit your shop regularly, and you read all of the specialist folk-music magazines, newspapers and fanzines. You should therefore be aware of any new folk band who appear to be making some waves on the scene, from live reviews and from the reviews of the album in question. If you receive a call or package from the band's 'record company' (perhaps offering a couple of CDs on sale or return), you'll therefore take up the offer. Some of your customers will already be interested, as they read the same magazines as yourself. When you receive the product, if you like it you'll recommend it to some more customers whom you think will also like it. You'll then re-order, and this time you'll pay up front.

If this seems like small potatoes, consider this: there is one band in existence (a folk band, as it happens) who – without any formal distribution and by using the methods above – distributed 2,000 copies of their debut album to dealers by mail order alone. Assuming that they cleared perhaps £6 per copy, after manufacturing and postage this would leave them with £12,000. They easily covered the cost of recording the album and their other expenses, and every subsequent sale after this point had been achieved earned them further profit.

How many new bands signed to traditional record deals can say that they achieved a profit on their first release?

overseas sales and the internet

If you have obtained the services of a distributor, he or she will be seeking to export your product to as many countries as possible. However, if you haven't been able to distribute your product, it doesn't mean that your records won't be available overseas. There are a number of exporters in the UK who may be interested in exporting your product overseas, particularly in specialist fields such as dance and rock, as they will have customers in overseas territories who are distributors, and who may specialise in your genre.

In addition, you may find that your web site receives dealer enquires, and the more 'niche' the musical field in which you operate the more likely this is. Remember that one of the great advantages of being an artist in the UK is that, if the UK press likes you and prints some favourable reviews, these will be read all over the world by both fans and people within the business. Similarly, overseas fans who learn of your band via your web site may be successful in persuading their local dealer to import some of your product.

Again, it's tempting to dismiss the few sales here and there outside the UK as being of little consequence, but you should be of the opinion that, at the end of the day, a sale is a sale and a fan is a fan, and that you can never tell where such sales may lead. For example, if you release a punk single in the UK, you may well be able to export a fair number of copies to Japan. There are two reasons for this: firstly, your UK distributor will have made their Japanese customers and contacts aware of the release, and some of them may wish to import any punk single, whoever the band; and secondly, specialist Japanese dealers may have bought your record via your web site. Although by no means likely, it's not impossible that the small amount of interest that your single will have generated may be enough for a Japanese label to become interested in licensing your album, should you decide to make one.

conclusion

You should proceed on the basis that your product will achieve distribution, as long as you present a distributor with valid reasons for getting involved. You should therefore research distributors from a very early stage, and approach them with advance product as soon as it's ready. In obtaining proper distribution you'll be entering a completely new arena, and you'll need to reconsider your entire approach to manufacturing and scheduling, and the marketing and promotion of the release itself.

marketing and promotion

E very flyposter you see on the street, most of the records you hear on the radio, every advert you see in the music press, and every band you see on TV is there as a result of the marketing and promotion undertaken by record companies and the people they hire to plug the records they release.

This chapter examines how you can copy the activities of a record company (albeit on a much smaller scale) in order to market and promote your own records. Now that you have been able to distribute your product, ensuring that it's available throughout the UK, and possibly overseas, your should focus on making as many people aware of your product as possible.

Needless to say, major record companies and the larger independent companies operate with marketing and promotion budgets that are huge in comparison to the minimal amounts of money that will be available to yourself. However, with some careful planning and a little forethought, a little money can go a long way. Remember that spending money on marketing and promotion should be seen as an investment; whatever you spend on increasing public awareness in your band and product should be more than recouped thanks to the increased sales that such marketing and promotion generates.

objectives

The main objectives of marketing and promotion are to increase awareness of a new release, thus stimulating sales, and to increase the general public's awareness of the band and its activities. It's therefore vital that you plan your marketing and promotion strategy as far in advance of release as possible, and set yourself achievable targets.

You will already have agreed on the best release date for your record with your distributor, be it an album or single. You'll need to allow yourselves at least three months before this date to build up public expectation of the record's release, and at least six weeks within that period to work with finished product. You can therefore work out the latest possible date on which you can be in possession of finished product, and work backwards from that date to establish the latest date on which you can start manufacturing stock (allowing some leeway for any hold-ups that occur at the factory or in the delivery process).

You should be aiming for the record to arrive on the shelves in the middle of a whirlwind (or at least a mild breeze) of activity. Accordingly, you should identify your goals early on, which should include, as a bare minimum, the following: touring and live reviews; published reviews; reviews in other media, such as web sites; advertising; radio play and TV exposure; local postering and flyering.

touring and live reviews

You'll need to organise some tour dates as early as possible, in order to coincide with the first few weeks of any record's release. If it's assumed that a single is unlikely to enjoy a significant amount of airplay, and an album even less, then hitting the road is the only way to take the music to the people. Dates should be constructed in two separate periods.

If you're gradually coming to the attention of the national music press, it's important to try your best to obtain a live review by playing a London show about four weeks ahead of the release date. If this show is reviewed, the review is likely to be printed two or possibly three issues later – in other words, the week before the release of the record. As part of your general research, you should be aware of the names of all the live reviews editors in the major music press, and they in return should be aware of the band. If they like the advance material you've sent them, or can at least appreciate its merits without thinking that it's the greatest single in the world...ever, then they'll certainly consider sending a reviewer down to see the show. It's important to stress that every music paper likes to discover new bands before their rivals, and it's wrong to assume that they are as cynical and jaded as record companies in their approach to new bands.

So hopefully you'll be able to secure a London show in a reasonably well-known venue about a month ahead of the release date, and hopefully there's a chance that this show will be reviewed. You should also play a few low-key shows around your local area over the preceding few nights to iron out any problems with your set, giving out flyers at each show which display news of the release, including details of the catalogue number and ordering information.

The second round of live dates will need to take place around the release date, ideally beginning late in the week of release. These dates should include a prestigious show in your home town, at a venue at which the band doesn't normally play, which can be staged as a kind of launch party for the release. You should also play other shows, in as many major cities as possible, and you should also perform a follow-up gig in London, which should have been plugged at your last show in the capital.

Much more detail on gigging and touring can be found later in this book, but it's important – in terms of the release of a record – that you book in dates for your band as early as is practical. If your distributor is aware of the dates fairly early on, this may persuade dealers in the towns in which you're playing to stock your records. Also, even if dealers are rather non-commital about stocking your product, the fact that you're playing in their town shouldn't escape their attention, and they will certainly be more aware of you when those who saw the gig try to order the record from them (hopefully!).

There is always a huge debate in the industry as to whether or not touring sells records. The answer is yes, it does, and particularly for a band in this kind of position. After all, unlike bands signed to a traditional record deal, a self-managed band can sell its own records at the show.

reviews in print

The most important thing to worry about in terms of published reviews is the concept of deadlines. You can't control whether you get reviewed or not, or whether your release is panned, but unless you're absolutely methodical in your approach to press reviews then you may not even stand a chance of being reviewed in the first place. Any review or editorial snippet can act as a piece of free advertising (the small cost of sending out material notwithstanding), and will hopefully provide you with choice of press quotes that you'll be able to use to promote the band for some time after the release.

You should already have a database of local and national music press and fanzines, and you now need to sub-divide it into the following sections: the local weekly or daily press; the regional weekly or daily press; the national weekly or daily press; the weekly music press; the monthly music press; and any other music publications. It is easy to establish the latest possible dates upon which material can be submitted for review by calling up the relevant journalists and reviews editors, and you can then work out a timetable for posting them your material. This may mean that you'll have to send some monthly or bi-monthly titles review copies of the album or single on CD-R or (less commonly now) cassette, but this shouldn't make a difference to their decision whether or not to review the product, as long as the advance copy is clearly marked with the release date, the catalogue number and the distributor, and is accompanied by the same press release and other information as the finished product.

A review package should comprise a copy of the review item (a finished CD, or an advance CD-R or cassette); a press release; a biography of the band; a picture of the band; and the front-sleeve picture or, if possible, an extra inlay card. Unlike a more general press release (perhaps informing people about forthcoming gigs), the press release that accompanies a review copy must be reasonably formulaic, and should include precise details of the release.

A press release for an album by our fast-rising combo Sanctuary might thus look something like this:

XYZ RECORDS
('Record label' logo and address)

SANCTUARY

Debut album: *Quasimodo's Revenge*

Sheffield's finest sons, **SANCTUARY**, release their long-awaited debut album, *Quasimodo's Revenge*, on XYZ Records on June 26th 2000.

The band have spent the last few months holed up in the studio with legendary producer Neil Gotrich, emerging with an album that's already being tipped as a future classic.

Quasimodo's Revenge captures the full-on power of the **SANCTUARY** live experience, and blends it with a new-found songwriting maturity borne of the partnership between vocalist Pete Rimadonna and guitarist Les Paul. From the explosive Zep-influenced opener, 'Seas Of Cheese', through to the delicate balladry of 'Camberwick Blue', the album is an intoxicating mix of funk and roll.

Says Rimadonna: "This album is everything we hoped it would be. Recording it was intense, but Neil [Gotrich] got the best out of us. I can't wait to get out on the road with the album and show how far we've moved on."

Sure enough, **SANCTUARY** mark the release of the album with a series of dates around the UK.

June 2000
29th   SHEFFIELD   (venue and details)
30th   BIRMINGHAM   (venue and details)

July 2000
1st   BRIGHTON   (venue and details)
2nd   LONDON   (venue and details)

The band will be announcing a full length UK tour for later in the year, as well as festival appearances.

Artist: **SANCTUARY**
Album: *Quasimodo's Revenge*
Label: XYZ Records
Distributor: Shellshock/Pinnacle
Cat No: XYZCD001
Format: CD only
Release Date: 26 June 2000

For further details contact: XYZ Records (address and contact details)/Decoy Publicity (address and contact details)

Attached: CD – *Quasimodo's Revenge*
          SANCTUARY biography
          Band photograph
          Inlay card artwork

As you can see, the press release is very upbeat, and supplies the journalist with some prepared quotes from the band which can be used in articles and reviews. If you have a number of supporters on the local press, you can expand on this area; for instance, if there is a particular journalist on a local paper who loves your band, you may be able to persuade him or her to write a full feature on you, maybe even providing him or her with a sneak preview of your record so that the piece can include a track-by-track review.

On a practical level, it's obviously going to be frustrating to spend time and money on sending out your review copies if your material doesn't end up being reviewed. You can cut costs as much as possible by buying jiffy bags in bulk from a wholesale stationery supplier, and by posting them second class (in which case, you should realistically allow a week for delivery).

You should call each targeted journalist or reviews editor a week or so after you have sent them your material, to make sure that they've received it and to find out if there will be a review forthcoming. There may already be one written, although it's unlikely that you'll be able to find out its content until it appears in the publication. If they show no interest in your music, you could ask for your review copy back, if you feel that this is appropriate – certainly from local journalists who clearly don't like your band.

Ultimately, a positive review in any type of publication, however obscure, is incredibly useful, and you don't have to be a major record label or PR company to ensure a review. There is at least one example of a band releasing a limited edition indie single through a small label and dealing with all of the regional press themselves. The reviews were great, including a 'Pick Of The Week' slot in a major regional evening paper, in preference to Gomez, Mel G and The Beautiful South. It can be done.

reviews in other media

You should be aware of any web sites which specialise in the musical genre in which you operate, and you should submit copies of the record for review to these organisations as soon as you can, and maybe even consider writing some reviews yourself and posting them on newsgroups or some other appropriate sites. Your own website should carry the best reviews of the album, of course, both in the press and by fans, perhaps with some choice quotes on the front page of the site.

Getting your music reviewed on Ceefax and other Teletext services is by no means easy, and sending review copies to these organisations is a calculated risk – you could be potentially wasting copies of your record that could otherwise be sold at gigs.

advertising

Placing an advertisement is significantly expensive, in almost any publication, and it's therefore important to ensure that you get the best value for money and as much exposure as possible. Assuming that your record is being distributed properly, you may find that your distributor regularly takes out an ad in the weekly music press, promoting forthcoming releases by bands with which he or she is connected. The cost of the ad is normally split between all of the bands and deducted from their sales income, but the amount paid for this is minimal when set against the exposure that such an ad will generate in, for example, the *NME*, particularly if the ad includes more than just a small picture of the record sleeve (a press quote, for example). Even if your distributor doesn't take out regular advertisements themselves, they will be able to tell you which publications are likely to have the most effect, and by which the dealers are most impressed.

If you decide to take out an advert yourself, you must ask yourself whether it's sensible to advertise in the weekly press (in other words, in next week's fish-and-chip paper) or whether there is a monthly title which, while having more expensive advertising rates, will be around longer and which their readers may keep for many months. This will largely depend on your band's musical genre; there are few major monthly titles that deal in anything other than mainstream rock and the more commercial end of indie (apart from magazines such as *The Fly*). It's hugely expensive to advertise in magazines such as *Q*, for the simple reason that they have hundreds of thousands of readers.

Your best approach is to be realistic, setting your sights low and finding out how much a small ad in the weekly music press costs. The ad you place should be as simple and as striking as possible, and should contain the following key elements: the release, including the catalogue number, the distributor and the release date, along with the inlay card design; the band's website address and postal address; the logo of your 'label'; any forthcoming tour dates; and one or two favourable press quotes.

Similarly, if you're only placing an ad in the 'live dates' section of the paper, this ad should also provide details of the address of your web site and the release itself, including the catalogue number and the release date, while concentrating primarily on the tour dates themselves. Also, be careful to ensure that you're up to speed with the artwork requirements and deadlines of each publication.

radio and TV

Exposure on the radio and on TV is a pretty straightforward area to cover – you're unlikely to get any significant radio play, and you're even less likely to appear on television. It's a shame to be so pessimistic, but it's unwise to be optimistic about achieving either, so that, if you manage to obtain any radio or TV exposure, it will be a welcome bonus.

As most people know, radio in the UK is divided into national, regional and local stations, which are controlled either by independent companies or by the BBC. National radio still features specialist shows (on Radio One, for example), which are receptive to new music outside the confines of the playlist. The major independent stations and the large regional stations have rigid programming policies, which aren't designed to allow the broadcasting of much independent music, if any. However, some adventurous local stations – both controlled by the BBC and independent – can still be receptive to local independent music, particularly if it's connected to a local event or news. However, the real issue is exactly how music is delivered to radio stations. Here, indeed, are shark-infested waters, where major record companies with powerful promotions departments, as well as independent pluggers, fight for every single place on the playlist.

If you're releasing an album, to a certain extent there is little pressure. Some key tracks may be played on local shows, or even the more left-field regional shows; if you're producing music in a specialist genre, and your product is of a high enough quality, you may pick up some plays is you plug the album to individual DJs and producers under the guise of your 'label'. It's almost certainly not worth employing a plugger, unless you have money to burn, or unless you're absolutely convinced that the plugger can deliver something (a live session, for example) that you cannot obtain yourself.

Pluggers, whether independent or employed by a record company, have one goal in life: to win exposure for their clients on the radio and television, and to convince opinion shapers (DJs, producers, presenters and moguls) that their client's new single is possibly the greatest record ever made. This task involves huge amounts of pleading, wheedling, lunches, freebies, lager and, possibly, drugs, in no particular order. Somebody once memorably described a plugger as 'someone you pay to tell you that nobody likes the record'. This may sound cynical, perhaps, but is all too often true. Pluggers operate on a fee structure which involves a fixed payment (either on a per-record or a per-month basis), plus bonuses according to chart positions or playlisting.

You won't be able to afford a plugger unless you have a really serious budget. You may be able to cut a moderate deal with a plugger (particularly a regional plugger) to handle a single release, but unless a significant amount of money changes hands you're probably paying him simply to send out your record to a few radio stations, and to make a few follow-up calls.

Television exposure is almost impossible to achieve, unless there are local cable or news shows which are receptive to either a live performance, or you can pull off a publicity stunt which will attract their attention on a slow news day. If you can manage to blag your way onto any kind of TV show, you should try to use the 'TV track' you've recorded so that the instrumentalists can mime along to a live vocal. This is because the actual sound facilities offered by local TV crews on an OB (Outside Broadcast), or even on a studio performance, are capable of making even the most powerful live performance sound as though it's being recorded through a cushion.

local posters and flyering

The release of your debut single or album should be accompanied by as much of a local fanfare as possible. This will not only potentially increase sales but will also give your local audience (and even people who haven't yet taken an interest in the band) the impression that you've taken an important step.

You should consider distributing posters and flyers which use the album cover design, rather than simply adding the release information to your existing flyers. The posters themselves may be useful as saleable merchandising items, which will help to recover the costs of their manufacture. Also, small, independent local record shops may be receptive to the idea of erecting a window or in-store display to promote the release, as long as you supply them with enough posters and inlay cards to do so.

making a video

It's not completely beyond the realms of possibility that you'll find yourself in a position where you can make a promotional video for the band, either for a single release or to accompany a key track from your album. However, broadcasters have extremely strict technical requirements relating to the format on which you deliver the finished master (even, that is, if you can find a local TV or cable show that will show your video).

If you can make a creative and visually interesting promo clip for relatively little money – and this could mean shooting it on Super 8mm film or DV, and then editing it on a domestic system or at a local college – then it may still have some uses, even if it is not broadcast. For example, local clubs may be able to show it on their in-house systems to promote forthcoming gigs or the release of the record; local record shops may also be able to show it; the video can be sent to promoters, who can then help to win live slots for the band; overseas licensees may look more favourably on your product if there is an accompanying video available; you may be able to use the video on your single or album by releasing an 'enhanced CD'; and, finally, it may be possible to use the video on your website. Evidently, then, a video is a luxury, but a potentially useful one. Don't expect to see it on MTV or *The Box*, however!

independent press companies

Many bands signed to major labels with an in-house press department still prefer to be represented by independent companies in their dealings with the press. Similarly, smaller indie labels prefer to use independent press departments to shouldering the cost of an in-house department.

Unlike pluggers (many of whom, it has to be said, will take on any old record just as long as they're paid), independent press companies and press agents are choosy about the acts they represent. Most operate under a system whereby they're paid a fixed monthly fee system, plus expenses. Their job is to ensure that important journalists, editors and publications are aware of the band and receive a constant flow of newsworthy information, photographs and reviewable material. As well as their everyday work (arranging interviews, press conferences, launches and overseas trips), they are also largely responsible for the artist's image in the press, and they also gather gossip and rumour concerning the artist.

Hiring your own independent press representative or company is an expensive business; however, deals can be cut if they like your band, and they're interested in building a long term relationship with you, as long as the band and their management are prepared to do a certain amount of the legwork themselves. In certain musical genres, it may be that independent press representation is the most important weapon in any new band's arsenal.

Such companies and individuals should be approached months before the scheduled release date of your album or single so that, if they decide to take you on, they stand a chance of whipping up public interest in your release.

conclusion

All record companies allocate a certain budget for marketing and promotion for every release, which is based on their projected sales figures and their overall hopes for a particular band. Such expenditure is a calculated risk, designed to achieve increased sales for a specific release and also to general increase public awareness of the band. It's important that you adopt the same approach, setting yourself some achievable goals and allocating a budget for marketing and promotion, right down to every last stamp and jiffy bag.

Realistically, you should be hoping to achieve some press reviews and editorial coverage, and employing some inexpensive and carefully-targeted approaches to getting your single played on specific radio shows. You should then follow this up by taking out some strategic advertising at around the actual release date to publicise the release and the touring activity that will go with it.

touring

Touring sounds a somewhat grand term for the gigging aspirations of any new band, and probably conjures up images of sleeper buses, articulated lorries groaning with backline and PA, and hordes of crew swarming around festooned with laminates and keys. Yet it's too easy to imagine that any band is simply confined to sporadic gigging in their home town and surrounding area unless some seismic change in their fortunes occurs.

For most bands and managers reading this book, the reality of gigging is likely to be along the following lines. You'll get a gig at your usual venue, or you'll support a band at another gig. You'll turn up in a fleet of cars or a battered Transit, containing backline that is close to meltdown, and load your gear into the venue, under the disparaging eye of the promoter and the sound man. You'll mooch around on the floor of the gig, surrounded by gear, waiting to soundcheck. Then you'll struggle onto a stage that's undoubtedly too small for one band, never mind three. You'll have to negotiate complex arrangements with other bands concerning borrowing their drum kit or guitar amp, and sorting out what will happen if anything breaks or blows up. Finally, you'll have a ten-minute soundcheck before you enter a dressing room which is full of other musicians, equipment and a strange, foetid smell, and yet contains no beer or food. You'll end up hanging around miserably as the previous band runs over time, bundle your gear onto the stage, and proceed to play your set amidst gales of feedback in front of an indifferent audience. Then you'll load out your gear, shout at each other, attempt to prise as much as a tenner from the promoter, fail, and go home.

A bleak perspective, for sure, but one that will probably be all too familiar. So what can be done to alleviate the torture of gigging like this, and turn it into a worthwhile opportunity?

are you ready to rock?

Too many bands inflict themselves on an audience before they are even remotely ready to perform live, and for a variety of reasons – out of an inability to be sufficiently self critical, for example, or laziness, or a lack of repertoire – but it's not enough to simply rehearse in front of an audience; you may not be 'professional' in financial terms, but your approach should be as professional as your resources will allow. As with recording, gigging is largely a matter of preparation, both creatively and in terms of maximising on all of the opportunities that may arise as a result of the gig.

You should ask yourselves some hard questions before deciding you're ready to play live. Have you actually got a set – if not a one-hour headline set, then at least a 30-minute support set – or are you simply going to play all of the songs that you know? Are you all well rehearsed, and does everyone know what they are playing, or do you harbour secret fears that the drummer will lose the plot completely after three songs and the gig will descend into a shambles? Is the set well paced and exciting, and is the frontperson confident enough and able to interact with the audience between songs, or are you just going to play song after song with the occasional mumbled introduction?

rehearsals

Regular rehearsals should be the cornerstone of every band's existence; they provide an opportunity not only to hone and improve existing songs but also to rehearse new ones, and to experiment with the order of the set. They also provide an opportunity for the band members to bond well, and a forum for the discussion of any other business. Any band serious about their career should be rehearsing at least once a week, with a regular time slot at their local rehearsal rooms that seldom changes. If any band members consistently have problems with rehearsals, turn up late, always have to leave early, or appear not to be taking this commitment seriously, then they shouldn't be in the band.

You should resist the temptation to spend the first half an hour of any rehearsal taking your time in setting up, having a fag and talking about the weather; instead, aim to get started straight away and have a break in the middle or at the end. Make sure that there is plenty of tea, coffee, water or beer on tap in the rehearsal room, and make the room as comfortable as possible for the short period that you're there. Always remember to take in a tape recorder with you and record the entire session, so that you can listen back to it during breaks or at the next session to fine-tune and perfect your performance.

If your next gig is very soon, spend the final part of the rehearsal running through the set with no breaks, easing off on vocals you think that the gig will suffer if your vocalist becomes croaky. If possible, the lead vocalist should always have a separate vocal rehearsal with any other vocalists in the band, preferably acoustically, in order to work out any harmonies you may wish to use and to experiment with variations.

You should also rehearse all guitar changes in real time, as you run through the set, working out where the frontperson may need to chat with the audience or where there may need to be a longer-than-usual guitar-free introduction to cover the gap between changes.

the frontperson

This sounds a bit PC, but what we mean is The Star, The Man, The Babe – ultimately, the person at which most people will be looking throughout the gig. In other words, the vocalist. If you're the person in question, the brutal truth is that the success of most bands in the traditional rock and pop formats (and also many dance acts) stands or falls largely on the strength of their frontperson or singer.

To a certain extent, this has nothing to do with vocal ability or general talent; we all know that Ian Brown is by no means the greatest singer in the world (no disrespect intended!), but he is indisputably a star, with a magnetic stage presence. Other bands, such as Gomez, present themselves as an ensemble, with the sum of their parts being more important than any individual member.

It's impossible to teach someone to be a star (as the old adage goes, you've either got it or you haven't), but there are many ways to bolster a front person's/lead singer's confidence. The first step is to ensure that their basic abilities are being used to their fullest extent, and here singing lessons – involving training in breathing, pitch control and projection – can transform a vocalist's abilities within a relatively short space of time. Image itself can be a source of significant anxiety, and it's vital for a frontperson to be confident with their look, posture and body language very early on. Also, on a general level, the frontperson needs to feel confident that the band behind him or her is competent, solid and exciting, so that he or she can concentrate fully on their performance.

It's also extremely important to focus on the rapport that the frontperson strikes up with the audience, and it may be that the frontperson feels more confident if they adopt a kind of persona that is an exaggerated and overblown version of their own personality. Without acting as if the band are playing at Las Vegas or Wembley Arena when in reality you're playing at the local arts centre, spoken introductions should be worked out carefully in advance, and should coincide with guitar changes and long musical introductions.

The frontperson, along with the rest of the band, should always have a contingency plan on standby in case a problem occurs with the equipment. This could take the form of cracking a few jokes, taking the opportunity to inform the audience about the band's information service, or even performing some songs acoustically if the snare decides to break or the bass amp fails.

troubleshooting

Try to remove any potential problems that may threaten the band as a stand-alone unit before they happen; a gig is no environment in which to wing it. If you're seriously worried about some of your equipment, you should see if you can borrow something more reliable. Always have spare guitar and bass strings, valves, leads, batteries and pliers to hand in order to perform impromptu maintenance, and it will help a great deal if you can persuade someone to crew for you for little or no money, however rudimentary their expertise.

Ensure that all your gear is flightcased, marked and insured, and keep a record of all your equipment's serial numbers in a safe place, together with the original receipts, if you have them.

how to get gigs

To many bands, who may be jealously scanning the pages of the *NME* and wondering why a certain band have wangled a particular support slot, or how another band can be headlining a London venue, actually landing gigs seems like some kind of magical art, requiring knowledge which mere mortals are forbidden, but this isn't actually the case. To be sure, at this point in the proceedings you should already be several steps ahead of other bands; you have your own album ready, a web site and a mailing list – in theory, an audience. If you've followed the advice I've given you so far, by this time you should be ready to rock.

A gig is staged by a promoter, who is someone (or, in many cases, an organisation) who stages a public event, such as a one-off concert or tour, and sells tickets for it. Promoters make their profit by spending less on the cost of staging the event than they receive in ticket revenue. This sounds obvious, but if you remember this you'll be able to concentrate on some factors which may be preventing you from getting booked. After all, why should a promoter stage a concert for you and cover all costs, even if you were performing for free, if he or she isn't going to earn any money on the deal? This can be reduced to the following question: how many people are going to pay to come and see you?

The band and the promoter both want the same thing: a packed gig that is safe, full of satisfied punters having a great night out, enjoyable and profitable. It would also be an added bonus to have a good take on the bar and to have everything running on time. Neither the band nor the promoter want to lose money, and it's disheartening for a band to play before a pathetic crowd, few of whom will bother returning to see the band again. Even so, too few bands take their relationships with promoters at the pub and club level seriously, which leads to a vicious circle of apathy, with the ultimate result that the promoter and the band end up blaming each other for a poor turnout.

All bands on the pub and club circuit need to work as hard as the promoter, or even harder, to make a success of each show, particularly if they sell their own albums and merchandise and if they expect to attract any media attention. When playing gigs, bands should have the following objectives in mind:

- Building a solid live following

- Generating media attention at a local and national level

- Selling merchandise and building a mailing list

- Staging entertaining performances and constantly improving their set

- Maintaining the profile of the band.

You'll notice that I haven't mentioned money. If you're gigging at pubs and small clubs just to earn money then you're destined to be skint; if you can cover your costs without making any compromises in your set then any profit you make on top should be treated as an unexpected and unlikely bonus.

Promoters like dealing with bands and managers who have a professional attitude. If you haven't dealt with the promoter of a particular club or pub or venue booker before, the best you can hope for is a support slot. Your best bet is to deliver a tape of your material to them and then keep calling them up until you actually get to talk to them. Try to act as confidently as possible, and first ask the promoter if he or she has had a chance to listen to the music. If not, you should still ask them if they have any support slots available over the next few months. (If they offer you something in the the next week or two, this won't give you much of a chance to arrange anything particularly impressive). You may be able to glean some useful information, and you may even get the promoter to promise that, if he likes the material, he'll give you a particular support slot.

Be prepared to talk about the band's influences and your album or single, and be confident about the number of people you can expect to attract to the gig, but don't exaggerate wildly – most small-time promoters would be very happy if a support band pulled in 30 people who wouldn't otherwise have attended the gig. Alternatively, you could pretend that you're assuming that the promoter will be prepared to give you a support slot, and ask him or her about the support slots he or she has available in a particular month early on in the conversation. If he or she mentions even one headline band that has a slot available, just ask straight away if you can have it, or if the promoter will pencil you in on the proviso that he will like the material.

Let's assume that, with a combination of sheer cheek and determination, you've been able to land some local gigs, perhaps of the calibre at which the band have already been playing. How can you guarantee their success?

staging successful gigs

(i) The Press

It may seem obvious, but few people stumble upon gigs by accident. The weekly music press and every concert listing in your area should be made aware of your gig, and provided with every last scrap of relevant information that they may require, from the time you'll be appearing on stage to the venue's phone number. After all, too much information is infinitely better than too little, and at the end of the day they'll only print what they need. It makes no difference that the promoter should have provided the same details to the same people; the band should also take it upon themselves to deal with the listings themselves.

If the venue has a regular advertisement in the local or national press, check and double check that they have spelled the name of your band correctly, find out if they'll also mention the address of your web site, and make sure that any special information (such as free CDs issued to the first ten people or drinks promotions) are also mentioned in the ad. You may even be able to have your band's logo featured in the ad, if you can persuade the newspaper to include it and take the trouble to drop off the disk at their offices or at their artwork house.

(ii) Posters And Flyers

You should already have printed some flyers, and perhaps even some posters, and you should deploy these at this point. Ensure that all of your flyers include the date of the gig and any extra relevant information, such as a reduced entry fee if the flyer is presented at the door, and that they are distributed in a strategic way rather than haphazardly spread around town. For example, you could advertise your gig next to adverts for gigs by other bands at the same venue, or in the same town, local record shops, pubs, colleges, music shops and so on. There's little point leaving hundreds of flyers in the local library or dropping them through doors.

It's important to emphasise the effectiveness of distributing flyers, as it not only promotes the gig itself but also increases the public's general awareness of the band. Additionally, on the night of the gig it gives promoters a good idea of which band on a multi-band bill has actually attracted the most numbers, rather than asking each member of the audience who they have come to see. You should view each flyer brought through the door as money in your pocket.

Posters should be displayed as early as possible, in locations where they stand a chance of staying on display for a reasonable length of time. You should certainly put them up at the venue where the gig will take place, and also in nearby pubs and colleges if you can obtain permission. Again, you'll only waste posters if you stick them up in an inappropriate area, as they'll be covered up or ripped down in a matter of hours.

(iii) Web Sites And Mailing Lists

You should begin plugging the gig on your web site as soon as the date is confirmed. If possible, use an eye-catching icon on the front page – you could change this as the date approaches. Similarly, you should e-mails everyone on your mailing list a few weeks before the gig, and then a few days beforehand, perhaps emphasising some updated information, such as a drinks promotion at the venue which you've held back until nearer the time.

Postal mailouts should be left until slightly nearer the time, and should always be accompanied by a reduced-entry flyer, in order to give people less chance of losing their flyer before the show.

You could also arrange a time before the show (just after the doors open for example) when anyone without a flyer can meet you and pick one up, perhaps arranging this to take place in a pub near the venue. After all, knocking £1 off the entry fee is a generous gesture, so it's worth plugging the flyer system as much as you can.

payment

Most pubs and clubs implement a variety of similar systems to ensure that they stand a chance of getting at least some money through the door, and – in theory, at least – pass some of it along to the band. All venues will be interested in recovering the costs incurred (from hiring the PA, the sound man, door staff and so on) from the gross profits before any split of the income is made.

It's unlikely that any promoter will offer you a flat fee, or a 'guarantee' at this stage (a fee that's guaranteed, no matter how many punters turn up. The usual arrangement in these circumstances is to give the band a split of the door takings after either an agreed sum of money has been taken, or a certain number for flyers. For example, a venue might agree that, after the first £150 has been taken on the door, the band receives £1 for every subsequent flyer that comes through. Alternatively, on a multi-band bill the venue may implement a percentage system, whereby the headline band receives the lion's share of the net income and the bands lower down the bill split the rest of the proceeds between them.

Many small venues and promoters operate without contracts, but it's best to establish the deal in writing in some form, even if this is by way of a one-line fax sent from the promoter.

dealing with the promoter

If you're unfamiliar with the venue or the promoter with whom you're dealing, it's advisable to go through a checklist with him or her on the phone. This list should be as exhaustive as possible while stopping short of being irritating, and should include:

- The precise address of the venue, its phone and fax numbers, the name of someone who can be contacted on the day, directions, and parking details. And if a map can be faxed to you, then so much the better.

- The get-in time, soundcheck times and stage times for all bands, not just your own

- Details of the dressing-room arrangements (how many rooms there are at the venue, for example, whether or not they're lockable, and whether or not there's anywhere to store your gear while the other bands are on stage)

- The provision of any catering arrangements (what's called a 'rider'), however basic, such as a beer allowance for the band or providing them with a meal

- The capacity of the venue, and details of all public transport likely to be of use to the audience

- Full details of the PA and backline arrangements that are available at the venue, as well as lighting arrangements, together with a contact number for the sound man

- At what time the venue imposes a curfew, and at what time your gear has to be loaded out, and whether you can load out before the end of the night if you're not headlining

- Whether or not you can sell merchandise at the venue, and if there's an area set aside for this. (Don't even suggest that there might be a charge involved for this!)

- Details of the local and national press whom the promoter will be providing details of the gig

- If the promoter be selling advance tickets, how much they will be, where they will be sold, and the price for entry on the door

- The allocated size of your guest list, and whether or not you can have more people on a reduced-price list.

When you've taken care of everything on your checklist, you're then in a position to work together with the promoter to check that everything is in place to make sure that the gig is as successful as possible. If this is the case, you should aim for a return booking as quickly as possible – diaries are quickly filled up, and in this case it's important that you strike while the iron is hot.

the day of the gig

If you have the opportunity to perform any last minute promotion then so much the better, but it's probably more important to make sure that all of the band members are aware of their own individual responsibilities. You should make sure that people are appointed to take care of the flyers and organise the merchandising area, someone should draw the short straw and be responsible for staying sober and driving the gear home, and someone else should be in charge of set lists (try to avoid scribbling these out in the dressing room just before you go on stage).

Do your best to make sure that you arrive on time, if not early, and then load in your gear and start setting up on the floor of the venue so that you can move onto the stage when your turn comes. if you have to move your equipment off the stage after your soundcheck, make sure that it's all stored securely, and try to make sure that the members of the band don't scatter their gear to the four winds until just before your slot. After this, arrange a time at which to meet back at the venue. From this point on, all of your partners and friends should be ignored as much as possible in order to give the band enough space to focus on the show.

You should also establish exactly what will happen as soon as the set ends so that everyone knows what they should be doing. Change these individual responsibilities within the band with every show will ensure that the same people don't get lumbered with the same tedious jobs all of the time. Someone should get the van, others should pack the gear ready for the load out, someone else should man the merchandising stand, and someone should be assigned to talk to the promoter about another show and to extract the cash from him or her.

Gigs are essentially ungovernable events, particularly hectic ones, and its easy for them to get out of control. If you make sure that a system is worked out in advance that will make sure that everything that is supposed to happen on the day happens at the right time, the sooner you'll be able to get to the bar after the show. And one final thing: someone should do an 'idiot check' of the stage and dressing room before you leave, just to check that nobody has left any gear behind or that any of it has been 'borrowed' by another band.

playing larger venues

With some time and application, and by paying attention to forging good relationships with local promoters, you should be able to establish yourselves on your local circuit and build an entourage of fans. You next goal should be to move this up a level, both in terms of the kind of gigs you play and the bands with whom that you appear.

(i) Supporting Signed Bands

Bands with a record deal (by which we mean those which are signed to a major or independent company and which have a released or scheduled product), and who are committed to touring, usually employ an agent to book gigs for them. Agents are responsible for liaising with promoters and venue bookers, and for booking shows for the bands on their roster. They operate in close co-operation with the manager of the band, and with the record company, in developing a touring strategy for the band that coincides with their product releases. This can take the form of a headline tour, where the support is likely to be offered to another of the agent's clients or a band signed to the same record company, or a support tour.

If the band in question is headlining a low-level pub or club tour, it should be possible for you to land yourself an opening slot, maybe third on the bill before the main support act plays. This is a decision that should be agreed upon by the local promoter (who should be singing your praises), the headline band's agent (who will be reluctant), the headline band's management (who may be more receptive if they are worried that their band may not draw in a full house) and the manager/agent of the main support act (who will be irritated, but ignored by everyone else).

If – by a combination of good timing, persuasiveness and cunning – you manage to obtain an opening slot for a signed band that is expected to pull in a decent crowd, you should be in a position in which you can afford to give yourself a pat on the back – before your work out how you're going to steal their audience.

You should expect the headline band's crew to give you a hard time at the gig, and don't assume that they'll let you use their sound man, change any of the settings on the desk, borrow even as much as a plug, have some of their beer or even use the dressing room, unless they seem receptive. Bands who are on the road, with or without the traditional glowering tour manager, are fragile things and don't like their touring schedule upset by some uppity local support band.

If you supply their sound man with a few beers, a T-shirt, a CD and £20 or so, this may smooth things along, but remember you should always remember that their name is on the ticket, not yours. Try to establish if any local (or indeed national) journalists are coming along well in advance, and then try to persuade them to get there early to catch your set. Be ready with some spare biographies and CDs in case there is anyone at the gig of any influence.

(ii) Special Events

If you're regularly headlining at all of the usual venues, you don't want to give the impression that you're simply doing the rounds every few weeks. Your audience will get bored and will stop coming, thinking that they'll be able to see you again in a short while.

You may need to consider performing less often, or (better still) staging a special gig at an larger or more unusual venue than usual. You could even hire in some more adventurous lighting and a more powerful PA, and attempt to create the impression that this gig is something special. It may be that the promoter with whom you regularly arrange things will be interested in moving things onto a more ambitious level, and you should always be looking for opportunities to surprise your audience with your next move in order to sustain their interest.

Although such events are more risky, in terms of the amount of investment involved, if they are promoted and staged professionally they can elevate the reputation of a band in its local area from 'good band' to 'local heroes'.

(iii) London Shows

You may have played a few shows in London where the entire focus of the evening was the hope that a certain A&R person would come to see the band, driven back up the motorway fuming at his or her inevitable non-appearance, and had a dreadful gig into the bargain. Consequently, you may imagine that, as you have effectively turned your back on the idea of getting a traditional record deal, it's less important to play regularly in London. This, however, is not the case at all; in fact, it's perhaps even more important.

Generally speaking, all aspects of the music business are almost entirely oriented around the capital. All of the major music publications and their journalists, distributors, lawyers, PR companies, promoters, agents, are London-based, as are the most important club venues. Just because you're taking the DIY route in terms of actually releasing your records, this doesn't mean that you should ignore London; you should simply approach it with a different perspective.

For the promoter, finding chances for an out-of town band to play gigs in London requires the same approach as a local gig, albeit with a few differences. You'll need to consider how to run a coach from your home town to London for the day (which can work out to be surprisingly cheap) and sell tickets to your supporters. Ticket sales may cover costs in itself, especially if the band's backline is small enough to fit onto the coach as well as the people.

You may be playing an opening slot (third on the bill) at the Barfly or the Dublin Castle, if the promoter likes your material and is convinced that you'll bring down a coach-load of supporters. This may sound less than prestigious, but is actually a lot better than it sounds. Your band will soundcheck last, your gear will stay on the stage, you'll finish early and therefore be able to get home. More importantly, being first on means that it's more likely that any industry people you need to see will be there.

If you're on the way to getting your record released, or even if it has already been released, you should get as much done on your one day in London as possible, while the rest of your supporters see the sights. If you're going to master your record in London, you may have time to do this before the start of the show. If possible, you should take the opportunity to meet up with your lawyer, try to set up meetings with PR companies (even if you haven't yet got one on board yet), or try to meet up with journalists, however small the publication for which they write. It may also be necessary for you to set up a meeting with your distributor, or to invite some of their staff to the show. While you have the opportunity, you could also meet up with London-based bands or their managers to determine if there's any the possibility of obtaining support slots in the future. Also, check out other venues for future reference, and pick up copies of overseas music publications that you may not be able to get at home – the list of useful things with which you can occupy your time in London is endless.

If you're considering hiring a coach, try to give fans as much advance warning as possible through your website and on any newsletters, so that you can gauge how many are likely to be travelling down to see the gig. Remember that people will need to book a day off if they are working. It's important to make the point at which people rendezvous with the coach as close to the venue as possible, so that people don't wander off into the city and miss the show.

If you can build up a legion of fans in London, and you start to attract the attention of the London-based media, then you'll be in a much better position to capitalise on this attention you get through actual record sales than the large number of other bands who are performing as many gigs in London but are basing their entire existence on whether they get signed as a result.

If you're realistic in your aims, and you concentrate on promoting your band, building your audience and perfecting your performance, gigging will become one of your primary sources of income, as a stand-alone band outside the mainstream music business.

chapter 8

the internet

The Internet is probably the most significant phenomenon to strike the music business since its inception. Until recently, the sale of music was entirely dependent on the sale of physical product, and the marketing of music on a global scale was the exclusive province of record companies. However, the ever-growing influence of the Internet looks set to change all of that.

In terms of communications, the music industry (and some would say music in general, never mind the industry) has been one of the first areas of leisure activity to derive enormous benefit from the free and uncensored content offered over the worldwide web. As little as ten years ago, discovering new music and finding out the latest news on favourite artists was a matter of waiting for the press to print something (assuming, of course, that one could afford to subscribe to numerous magazines).

New artists and new music are already reaping enormous benefits from the Internet, whilst the record companies are struggling to come to terms with it. Net-based record labels are springing up all over the world, and product is finding a truly global audience. The only downside from this explosion of activity might possibly be that there is simply too much information available, and new bands risk being drowned in a tidal wave of competition, all clamouring for the attention of the global audience.

However, for the first time fans can now swap information about great bands with each other with the flow of information unencumbered by the record companies. Also for the first time, the bands themselves can communicate directly and cheaply with their audiences – only a few years ago, a major band's fan club office would have been subsumed by a sea of envelopes, newsletters and stamps, whereas now an ever-increasing number of fans simply use email. In the event of a change in release date, for example, or an addition of a tour date, or if the band have a TV appearance, the use of email has revolutionised the speed at which fans get the news.

The use of official band sites has also meant that misleading and inaccurate press stories can be refuted immediately, and in certain events the band can respond directly to points raised on the site. Webchats and webcasts of live gigs or studio sessions have become commonplace, and it's becoming the norm to give fans sneak previews of as-yet unreleased recordings.

An active and entertaining website will also serve to fill in the gaps between the release dates of official product. In the past it wasn't uncommon for months or years to go by without a single snippet of information appearing about a particular band.

Although record companies initially reacted with horror at the idea that their bands might be able to build a direct relationship with their audiences, common sense is finally beginning to prevail and many band sites now work in conjunction with the band's official page on their record company's site. More and more record labels are making their band's music available for download, at a price, and there is certain to be intense debate about exactly how much money per track will be good value whilst still preserving the intrinsic value of music. At the time of writing, the typical price of downloading a track by a known artist via an official site ranges from $1 to £1, although already a number of small labels are offering their tracks for less than this.

It's likely that, in the near future, there will be official download charts administered by the same organisations which currently administer the retail charts, and there will almost certainly be officially-recognised industry awards for the Internet sales of individual tracks. In the USA, it's commonplace for 'singles' released to radio and TV not to enjoy a retail release at all, with their chart placings being determined mainly by the amount of airplay they receive. The same thing is likely to happen to the charts worldwide, with the addition of download figures into the mix of sales.

Record companies are currently preoccupied with the question of whether the exploitation of music via the Internet will lead to the death of the album. The argument runs that people don't necessarily want to spend £15 or so on a collection of ten tracks, only to find that they only like a few of them. Because of the high profit margins built into the retail sales of albums, however, record companies are sure to resist this heavily, perhaps by limiting the number of single-track downloads from a particular artist in the hope of encouraging fans to purchase the whole album. It seems certain, however, that the overall cost of purchasing music will go down, and this has serious consequences for everyone in the music business. Record retailers will be threatened by record companies and bands cutting out the middleman and selling direct to their audiences, and record companies may also be unable to preserve the margins they have long enjoyed as pressure increases for standardised worldwide prices on the Internet. Artists' royalties may also decline in real terms, as the prices on which they are calculated fall.

Although people will always want to visit record stores, smaller retailers are inevitably going to be vulnerable due to the fact they can't possibly stock an enormous range of titles. On the other hand, massive record stores may well find that there is absolutely no need to carry huge stocks, and will instead offer online purchasing and instore listening, supported with rapid delivery.

So how can a new band take advantage of the Internet?

the band website

The starting point has to be the launch of a website for the band, however basic this may be. Your first decision will have to be the name of the site, and you will have to decide whether you wish to have either a non-virtual domain name, with which your site will be an extension of your web host, or your own virtual domain name, which is more expensive.

If you can afford it, it's a much better idea (and much more permanent) to register your own virtual domain name. If you search the Internet and discover that your band name has already been taken, you may have to do some lateral thinking and combine your band's name with additional words, or adapt it in some other way.

the functions and content of the site

The main functions of the site should be fourfold:

• To provide entertaining and useful information and news about the band to fans and curious visitors

• To sell the band's products, such as CDs and merchandise

• To provide a contact forum for business enquiries relating to the band and its products

• To provide a forum for fans to discuss the band and to interact with them, and to allow the band to communicate directly with its fans.

Designing and maintaining an effective and entertaining web site has never been cheaper or easier. If you have access to a fairly powerful PC and a scanner, and you're reasonably computer literate, you can design and build a site yourself using readily available web-page-creation software. Alternatively, there are usually professional or semi-professional web site designers in most areas who will be able to build your band's site for a variety of budgets, and it continues to become less and less expensive to hire a designer.

Whether you construct the site yourself or you decide to hire in an expert, the content of the site is what will either make it or break it. There are certain basic elements that every site should contain in order to maximise its effectiveness.

the homepage

This is the first page that visitors will see, and should therefore be striking and yet quick to load, which may rule out the use of photographs or banners. It should contain the band's logo, with perhaps a brief message or slogan (a favourable press quote is a good idea) and the Enter button.

the news page

The news page is the second page that visitors will see, and the most important. All the other pages of your site should be presented as buttons either above or to the side of this page. It should be kept updated regularly, because at least some visitors will wish to bookmark it, and (depending on how sophisticated you want to get) an animated icon on this page will be effective, perhaps one promoting a forthcoming gig. Similarly, if the site contains news of a release, you may wish to provide a link to the CD Sales page. (This page will be covered later.)

the biography page

You should put at least one picture of the band on the biography page, which should also contain details of the band members and their roles within the band, and the text should be more elaborate and more detailed than your standard band biography used for promotional purposes. If the biog refers to certain tracks, you may wish to provide a link to the Music page. (This page will be covered later.) Remember that, if more than one picture is used visitors may grow bored and go elsewhere.

pictures

That said, however, a good selection of band pictures is essential, especially for new visitors who are unfamiliar with the band. Some good live shots, preferably showing packed venues, will certainly give the impression that the band are big news in their local territory. Similarly, a good selection of studio shots will be revealing and also useful for journalists wishing to download them for use in their articles. You should also show another side of the band by including some everyday pictures. Again, it's important to keep this page regularly updated, and perhaps ask fans to email in their own pictures of the band.

music

This page should offer a good selection of RealAudio or MP3 tracks from the band, or even excerpts of tracks. You should also consider including some live recordings, if they are of a high enough quality. It's important to include the copyright details of each song (in the case of our imaginary band, Sanctuary: "Written by [name]. Arranged by Sanctuary. ©[year]. Copyright control, all rights reserved"), and also for the recordings themselves. This should read: "The copyright in all recordings is owned by Sanctuary. ©[year] Sanctuary, all rights reserved." The Music page should include a link to the CD Sales page.

the message board

Your site should also have a message board, or Guestbook page, on which fans can leave messages for the band and for each other. In time it may be possible for you to arrange webchats on this page, but in the first place it's probably best to design the page so that a series of strands can be seen, such as "When Is The Band's Next Gig?" In this way, fans can leave messages and receive replies which all visitors can see.

The message board should also be the place where fans can sign up for the information service, either by email or by emailing you their regular postal address so that you can write to them by post. You should also provide reassurances on this page that you won't pass on their address to third parties.

press and reviews

The Press page should contain any and all reviews that the band have picked up (only the good ones, of course!), which should either be scanned in their original form or retyped in plain text. This page could perhaps be headed with some choice press quotes, and divided into groups of live reviews and CD reviews. Fans could also be invited to submit reviews of gigs via email, although you may be asking for it if you suggest this!

interviews and diaries

It's a good idea to have an interview with the band on the site in order to provide fans with an insight into the personalities that make up the band. Many music publications, such as *NME* and *Q* have standard interview formats, which you can adapt or combine for your own purposes rather than go for the more traditional interview, in which the band simply discusses how they got started and their favourite foods. These interviews should be changed around regularly, perhaps concentrating on different members of the band.

If the band are hard at work in the studio or on tour, or are involved in any kind of event which may warrant a special mention, such as a festival, it's worth providing a special diary or an article to cover the event, or even asking the fans to submit their own material.

the shop

This is the sharp end of the site, where punters can buy CDs and merchandise by mail order directly from the site. Customers will wish to purchase either by credit card or by sending you either a cheque or postal order, or International Money Order, for the price of the product plus postage and packing.

Payment by credit card deserves special mention at this point. Although customers are becomes less wary about shopping online using their credit cards, it can be prohibitively expensive for you to set up a merchant account with your bank or building society so that you can take credit card orders directly. The solution is to use any one of the numerous credit card processors currently available, such as www.thenexus.co.uk or www.ccnow.com, who will take the orders for you, process the payment and mail you a cheque for the purchase price less their commission. Such services will send you an email every time they take an order, so that you know where to send the product.

For regular sales by mail, the page needs to consist of a basic order form that can be downloaded and posted to the band along with payment. It should look something like this:

ORDER FORM

Please send me the following:

ITEM	PRICE	NUMBER	TOTAL PRICE
Sanctuary Mini Album	7.99		
Black XL T-Shirt	12.00		
Black L T-Shirt	12.00		
Grey Skinny T-Shirt (One Size)	14.00		

COMBINED TOTAL............................

POSTAGE AND PACKAGING (SEE BELOW)............................

GRAND TOTAL............................

POSTAGE AND PACKAGING RATES

Per CD: UK £1.50/Mainland Europe £2.50/Rest Of World £4.00
Per T-Shirt: UK £2.00/Mainland Europe £4.00/Rest Of World £6.00

YOUR DETAILS

Name ....
Street Address ....
Town/City...
Country ....
Postal/Zip Code..
Email Address ....

Send your completed order form to: SANCTUARY, PO BOX 1672456, SHEFFIELD SG1 8DB, UNITED KINGDOM.

Payment is accepted in sterling (£), cheques, postal orders and international money orders. Please allow 28 days for delivery from receipt of order.

The page should ideally include pictures of all the items on offer, together with a few animated icons, such as a 'selling fast' (or hopefully a 'sold out') icon. You could also provide a space on the order form for fans to request specialist material, such as a CD that has been signed by the band.

business enquiries

A page should be set aside for business enquiries, which should simply state something like the following: "To enquire about booking the band for a live show, for licensing enquiries relating to the current album and future product or for export and distribution enquiries, please email us at [email] or fax us on [fax number]. Business enquiries only, please. Sanctuary are managed by [details], to whom all enquiries should be directed in the first instance."

You can certainly elaborate on the above for your website, but you should ensure that all aspect of the site remain entertaining, informative, visually interesting and quick to load.

marketing and promoting the web site

The website itself needs promoting as much as the band, as it provides a shop window to the world, and this can be of enormous help to your career. As a general rule, the website should always be promoted as the best place to find out information about the band, and the following methods to promote your site 'on the ground' will help achieve this.

on the ground

- The website address should always appear on flyers and posters

- It should also appear on all band-headed paper, business cards, and on emails sent by the band

- Band newsletters should feature the site heavily

- The website could be stencilled onto some or all of the band's flightcases

- You could use the website address as a stand alone T shirt design

- When the site is launched it should be the subject of its own press release to encourage local journalists to print the address.

on the net

(i) Search Engines

If you have the time, there are almost unlimited opportunities to promote your site. The site should be registered with all of the major search engines, and optimised by using keywords. You should to consider the title of the site properly when doing this, and avoid loading the title page with unnecessary keywords or you will be deluged with spam emails. The aim is to drive relevant traffic to your site, not just traffic for its own sake.

The main search engines – Alta Vista, Excite, Go.To, UK Plus, Yahoo, Webcrawler, InfoSeek, Lycos, Hot Bot and Deja.Com – account for the vast majority of searches, although there are many less relevant search engines with which you could also register.

(ii) Newsgroups

The number of newsgroups on which you could post messages urging people to visit your site is almost limitless, be they general discussion groups relating to your genre of music or newsgroups relating to specific bands. It's unwise to blatantly plug your site, as to do would be to run the risk of irritating people enough to spam you into oblivion, but a few subtle mentions may give rise to some visitors.

It's probably best to use newsgroups exactly for the purpose for which they were designed, as a place to debate and exchange news about certain artists or genres, and if in engaging in these discussions you can gently draw attention to your site then so much the better. It may well be the case that you pick up information on similar bands, labels and distributors while building up a list of relevant newsgroups, and this can be incredibly useful.

It's also probably much more beneficial for you to use newsgroups in a personal capacity, rather than blatantly as a member or manager of a band which you are trying to plug. You could initiate debates on the best new bands you have seen lately, for instance, mentioning your band within a host of perhaps better-known names.

(i) Other Band's Sites

There is some merit in leaving messages and links to your site on the sites of other bands, as long as you're subtle. You'll probably already be aware of a number of bands with whom you're often compared, and you should visit both their official sites and their fan sites. As well as being useful on a general level, and being a useful place to find inspiration for your own site, the sites of other bands can be a useful place to promote your own site in a variety of ways, both blatant and subtle. The most blatant method is to sign the band's guestbook or discussion page with a message bordering on the sad, such as going to Supergrass' site and writing: "Hey! If you like Supergrass, you're bound to like Sanctuary! Visit us at…"

It's better to concentrate on emphasising that your band are in roughly the same genre as the band on whose site you are posting messages, and it may be a good idea to include a line of a press review in your message. For example: "If you like it powerpoppy and punky, come and see why the *Sheffield Evening Post* said about Sanctuary 'the band are clearly the bastard sons of Supergrass and Happy Mondays'", followed by a link to your site.

(iv) Banner Ads And Reciprocal Links

It's highly unlikely that an ad banner for your site placed on another site will drive much traffic towards your site, even if that you can afford to advertise in this way in the first place. However, creating an ad banner and persuading fans of your site to place it on their own may be help a little, but it's unlikely to radically increase the traffic to your site. Also, if these other sites take your banner they will actually be encouraging people to leave their own sites, which doesn't strike me as a particularly good idea!

Reciprocal links to friendly sites (for example, those run by similar bands, or fans of your genre of music) can help to build up the levels of traffic to your site, as long as you take care not to overload your site with too many links.

new music sites

The last couple of years have seen the launch of an increasing number of sites aimed specifically at promoting new music and unsigned bands. Some are general sites, such as www.channelfly.com, which is allied to London's well-known venue The Barfly and *The Fly* magazine, and aimed particularly at independent live music.

Another very useful site is run by The Bands Register (www.bandreg.com), which keeps a huge database of band's names as well as details about them. The site also has a facility for A&R men to register with the site and receive recommendations on acts, and The Bands Register also releases its own CD compilations featuring unsigned bands which they think have commercial potential.

Recently there have been a huge number of sites launched which feature new music available for download. These sites tend to operate by providing each band with a page on their site which contains some biographical information and some RealAudio tracks that potential customers can hear, and they also allow the customer to purchase certain tracks by downloading them or having them delivered on a custom CD. The sites usually offer bands a share of the purchase price of each track, which usually works out at about 50%, after taking some deductions have been taken from the top. Sites such as Peoplesound (www.peoplesound.com) and Vitaminic (www.vitaminic.com) have implemented huge advertising budgets in order to attract bands to their sites, and to persuade the public to take a look. Peoplesound have even offered bands a £100 advance against their share, and have published charts in the weekly music press which provide details of which band's material is being downloaded the most.

The promotional potential of these sites is obvious, and signing up to one (or indeed all) of them can do a new band no harm whatsoever. There have been no figures published yet concerning the number of visitors each such site has received yet, although there have been some scarcely believable numbers bandied about. There are also no figures available concerning the amount of income even the most popular band has received.

It may be that, in the short term, only a few of these sites survive. The music industry has traditional exhibited mild disinterest at best, and downright scepticism at worst, about the benefits of such sites. They cite the fact that, on the bigger sites, there seems to be a certain lack of quality control in terms of which bands get picked for exposure on the site, which reduces their credibility. In addition, quotes from respected figures in the industry about the qualities of a particular site have – on certain occasions, at least – probably been due more to the fact that the person in question is being paid a retainer by the site or has been given some kind of consultancy or share options.

The smaller sites, such as Brandnewmusic (www.brandnewmusic.com) and Musicunsigned (www.musicunsigned.com), may have a better chance of fostering some new and interesting acts, because they operate with a stricter A&R policy.

In the medium term, it is likely that such sites will become more competitive with each other, in terms of the proportion of income which they pass on to their bands – indeed, some are already offering a 75% share. It may be that bands will be required to sign exclusive deals sites on which their music is available for a certain period of time. It seems inevitable that at least some of these sites will end up launching fully-fledged record labels and sign the most popular bands on the site. Such labels may run the risk of being too diverse, and their employees perhaps may not have the best traditional music business expertise, however, and they may find it difficult to enter into mainstream music.

Some sites may also have different agendas, such as setting up publishing companies to offer their bands deals rather than releasing records. One site already taking the publishing route is Popwire (www.popwire.com).

On the whole there is little or no downside to signing a deal with any number of these sites, provided that you (or your lawyer) read the contract in detail. It's probably unwise to imagine that you'll generate significant income from exposure on such sites, and if some does come your way then you should consider it a bonus. On the whole, these sites should be viewed as welcome promotional tools which may not be around forever.

merchandising

The sale of merchandise plays a vital part of every working band's income, and there's no reason why it shouldn't figure in your plans on a smaller scale. Merchandising is one of the investments you can make in product to sell which should return a healthy profit, if managed correctly.

Any band which gigs regularly and has a growing mailing list of supporters, as well as an active website, should strongly consider selling merchandise, both to earn income and to promote the band and (on occasion) goodwill. Merchandise has been growing steadily more sophisticated, and now it's not uncommon for major bands to sell items such as lighters, mugs and mouse mats in addition to the more commonplace T-shirts and sweatshirts.

A new band should have modest ambitions in terms of the type of product it can afford to manufacture and sell, as merchandising always requires a significant investment before any income trickles in. Before committing to manufacturing merchandise, it's prudent to get some kind of figure about sales which are absolutely guaranteed (to friends and fans, for example), and to calculate if you can break even straight away on money earned from these sales.

It's always cheaper to manufacture merchandise in large quantities, as you will get a discount for bulk orders which will vary according to the manufacturing/merchandising company you use. Although it may be tempting to obtain a discount of 50 pence per shirt on an order of an extra 50, for example, you should be careful not to overstock unless you have a large number of gigs lined up, or you have a guaranteed pre-sales figure.

It's also common sense to be aware of the time of year it'll be when you'll be selling the bulk of your merchandise; although T-shirts are popular all year round, your sales may founder if you embark on a series of summer shows and sell mainly fleeces and sweatshirts.

t-shirts

T-shirts are usually the mainstay of most band's merchandise catalogue. Resist the temptation to have only the most basic-quality T-shirts produced, as these will fade quickly, be poor value, and not do the band's reputation any good at all. After all, the same people will hopefully be coming to your gigs time and time again, and it won't be pleasant to watch a sea of black T-shirts gradually turning grey and shapeless, topped off by the faces of disgruntled fans.

You should choose good-quality, heavy T-shirts (Hanes and Screen Stars are both reputable names), and be extremely careful when choosing colours and sizes – some companies charge slightly extra for XL and XXL shirts, or for non-standard colours. It's not a particularly good idea to select colours that are too unusual or left-field, with a view to making your shirts 'different'; people are reasonably conservative in what they will buy in the way of merchandise, and your T-shirts should be primarily black or some other dark colour. However, every genre of music has different requirements, so it's impossible to generalise; it's a case of really knowing your audience and observing what they already wear, both in terms of regular clothes and merchandise of other bands. It's unwise to assume that your audience are all fashion victims and totally *au fait* with the current year's colour, unless you want to be left with boxes of taupe shirts with a ginger trim.

Whether a shirt will sell or not will be largely determined by the design. It's often a good idea to include a back-print design, and this can be obtained for the small extra cost of making a separate screen. Not only does a back print make each shirt seem better value but it also allows the shirts to be displayed in a more attractive manner on the merchandise board. If the shirt is designed to accompany a specific tour, it's traditional to include the tour dates in the design on the back of the shirt. (If the towns look impressive but the names of the venues don't, include only the names of the towns and the dates). You should avoid using designs which are controversial, possibly offensive or directly based on designs owned by other companies, who may have more expensive lawyers than you.

The more colours you incorporate in the design the more expensive the shirts will be. Unless you have a striking and particularly arty album, or a single cover shot that can be used for the T-shirts, it is best to avoid using photo shots.

If you have a number of female fans, you should also consider producing some shirts in girls' sizes and styles, such as skinny T-shirts. It's also a good idea to mix crew-neck and V-neck styles of shirts, if this can be accomplished at no extra cost.

sweatshirts

Sweatshirts have generally become less popular than they used to be, and it's difficult to have good-quality items produced at a reasonable price. You should maybe consider having V-neck shirts or polo shirts made as an alternative, perhaps with a small embroidered logo (which will cost significantly extra) as opposed to a print.

Another increasingly popular alternative is the embroidered fleece, and this can be either of the half-zip or full-zip variety. Although these are considerably more expensive to produce than sweatshirts, they're quality items which may appeal if your audience is the sort that's prepared to spend up to around £20 for clothing merchandise.

other items

Unless you're absolutely sure that you have such an ardent following that they'll buy almost anything, it's extremely unwise to divert from the traditional selection of clothing sold by most bands. Novelty items are unlikely to sell, especially promotional pens, mugs and so on, which most people will view as items of low value and expect to be given away.

Similarly, a new band won't be able to get away with selling items that larger, nationally-recognised bands can. The audience will be perfectly prepared to consider buying Oasis hats, for example, as everyone knows who Oasis are, but more obscure bands should restrict themselves to producing more traditional merchandise.

selling merchandise

There are two main avenues for selling merchandise: through a website or mailing list, and on the road. Both require a completely different approach.

mailing lists and web sites

A full list of merchandise should always be sent out with every newsletter issued by the band, preferably accompanied with pictures of the logos used on each shirt and detailed descriptions of the garments themselves. The merchandise list should also have an order form attached to it.

It's always best to provide the fullest possible descriptions possible of each item on offer, without going over the top. Rather than just say 'Black XL T-shirt with band logo on front', a more marketable phrase would be: 'High-quality black XL T-shirt in 100% cotton, with full-colour band logo front print'. You could even state name of the shirt's manufacturer in order to reassure people that they aren't buying an obscure brand.

The merchandise page on the website allows enormous scope for displaying inventive design ideas. It could feature pictures of band members or fans wearing each item of merchandise, perhaps accompanied by icons to attract attention such as 'Few Left!' or 'New!' Even if the items have sold out, it's still a good idea to keep them up on the page with a 'Sold Out' icon next to them, which will give the impression that people should be quick off the mark if they want to buy.

You should also ensure that the band's home page uses icons next to the merchandise page in order to indicate any changes or new items, and remember to email the people on your mailing list when new items become available or are nearly sold out.

sales at gigs

Selling merchandise to an audience at gigs seems like a fairly simple undertaking, but there are many ways in which can maximise the effectiveness of your approach to this. When booking a gig, it's extremely important to establish the following points with the promoter right from the beginning.

- Is it permitted for the band to sell merchandise at the gig, or does the venue insist on using its own staff to sell the merchandise and then deduct a commission from the sales proceeds?

- If the band are permitted to sell their merchandise themselves, is there an area of the venue set aside for this purpose. If so, what are its dimensions? Also, are there any power points nearby?

- Does the venue still take a commission if the band sell the merchandise themselves, and is the commission less than it would be if the venue's staff sold the items themselves. If not, why not?

- If you're supporting another band, do you need to obtain their permission to sell your merchandise? If you do, who is their manager, agent, tour manager or merchandise person?

Many venues charge a commission on sales of up to 25% of the gross price, or a fixed fee calculated on audience numbers. This is often 'justified' by the fact that they are providing people to sell the merchandise and/or a special area. You may have to consider increasing your prices in venues where such a commission is imposed.

Operating under the assumption that you can sell your merchandise from a good location and with little difficulty, you will then need to consider how to present the merchandise in the most attractive way. After all, you wouldn't consider buying clothes from a dilapidated shop with all of the stock in bin liners in unlit corners, so you should pay serious attention to the problem of how best to display your merchandise.

Initially, you'll need to build a basic but sturdy merchandise board, upon which T-shirts, CD inlays and posters can be pinned. A cheap way of building one of these is to use two folding wallpaper tables, bolting them together to create a large folding board. This can either be laid on its side in a 'V' shape and mounted on a table, or propped upright against a wall if the tables are made rigid once extended, using basic door bolts. The underside of the tables should form the outer side of the board when displayed, and the entire area should be covered with cork tiles or some other material in which pins can be stuck. In this way, when the tables are folded back together, the merchandise display will be kept safe in position inside the table, ready to be used at the next gig.

You should also carry some small clip lights on long leads to illuminate the display, and perhaps consider using ultraviolet bulbs, as they will make light colours fluoresce. You should attach one or more laminated A4 boards attached to the board, each clearly displaying the price of each item and other relevant details, such as to whom cheques should be made payable.

Ideally you should have someone there specifically to sell merchandise throughout the show. If this impossible, the stand should be left on display in a secure place with a notice informing people that merchandise will be on sale after the show. The stand should always be placed somewhere where it will be easily visible, but be careful not to position it in a tight corner, or this may prevent people from reaching it easily if the show is particularly well attended.

Always provide your salesperson with a float of cash to begin with, consisting of plenty of £5 notes and £1 coins. All stock should be counted at the start of the evening and again at the end to ensure that there are no discrepancies in the sales. The salesperson should always wear a one of the T-shirts for sale, which should, of course, be in impressively pristine condition.

It's easy for merchandise of any kind to be trashed in the hectic and beery atmosphere of a gig, whether it's CDs or garments, so it's wise to keep it in its own flight case, making sure the interior is spotless.

freebies

There will be many occasions on which people will expect a free T-shirt in return for some real or imagined favour, and this is particularly true of friends and relatives who may have helped out the band over a long period of time. This is only to be expected, and you may end up giving away quite a high percentage of your first run of T-shirts, just breaking even on the profits from the sale of the rest.

You may decide to give away a certain number of shirts, and if you do you should make a list of the people who deserve one before you even commit to manufacturing them. In this way you'll be able to calculate how many you need to produce in order to recoup the cost of the free shirts from sales of the rest.

The offer of a T-shirt which has cost you around £4.50 may generate goodwill that is priceless, so you need to be reasonably open-minded in your approach to giving away freebies in the early stages of your band's career. Whether the recipient is a promoter, a journalist, a manager, part of another band's crew, the owner of a record store or a DJ, in the music business the free T-shirt is an accepted form of currency.

licensing

You may have heard the word licensing and been unsure of its implications. In essence, a licensing arrangement is a deal which is made by an owner of rights (such as the rights in a recording) with a third party (another company or person), whereby that party is granted permission to exploit the rights in some way. For example, a UK record company which owns a band's album on a worldwide basis may not have the necessary resources or personnel to release that album itself in Japan, but by constructing a licence deal with a Japanese record company the UK company can then have the album released in that country without even having its own operation there.

With this example, the practicalities of such a deal would operate in the following way. The UK company would agree to the terms of a licence deal with the Japanese company, and as such the UK company would be referred to as the 'licensor' and the Japanese company as the 'licensee'. The terms of such a deal would almost certainly involve the Japanese company agreeing to release the album and then paying a royalty on the sale of each unit to the UK company. This royalty would be based on either the retail price of the records sold or the published dealer price, or on a formula combining either of these prices along with various deductions, resulting in a 'Royalty Base Price'.

The UK company would then expect to receive an advance against the above royalty, payable on the delivery or release of the album in Japan, or in instalments. No further monies would be paid over by the Japanese company until such an advance had been recouped from the royalties due on the sales. The dates upon which the Japanese company would be required to account to the UK company (ie the providing of royalty statements and payment) would also be agreed, and this would probably be every calendar half-year.

The agreement would also contain provisions, determining how long the Japanese company could have the rights for the album before the rights reverted back to the UK company (five years, for example), as well as more minor provisions. For example, the Japanese company may well be granted a 'sell-off' period after its exploitation term ended, within which it would still be permitted to sell its remaining stock of the album.

Upon signature of the deal and payment of the advance, the UK company would be expected to supply the Japanese company with the masters of the album and the original artwork on disk or film.

The artist would receive their royalties on sales in Japan from their UK company, at the contractual rate which they had agreed with their company for Japanese sales. This could be expressed as a straight royalty rate (which would be almost certainly lower than the rate the band receives on UK sales), in which case the only consideration is that the Royalty Base Price stated by the band's record contract should mirror the definition contained in the licensing deal which their record company has struck with the Japanese company. To use two different prices is a recipe for confusion and delays in the accounting process. Alternatively, a 'net receipts' provision would be in place, whereby the artists would receive a straight percentage of the monies which had been actually received by their UK company.

The only inherent danger in such arrangements – apart, of course, from the licensee doing a bad job in releasing the album and achieving less sales than had been hoped – is that two entities must now pay up before the artist sees any royalties. In other words, the Japanese company must account correctly to the UK company before the UK company can then account to the artist. This approach seems straightforward (if one assumes that both companies are intrinsically honest), but trouble may occur if the licensee has paid an overall advance to the licensor for the rights to several albums and such advance is 'cross-collateralised' (ie royalties arising from sales of all of the albums are allocated to paying back the whole advance). If the artist's album has sold well, but the licensee has not paid the record company because they are still waiting for their overall advance to recoup, then the artist will be relying on his or her UK company for payment on those sales using other income. This should be fine – as long as they have the money.

Major record companies effectively operate their own internal licensing arrangements, whereby a record made and owned by Sony UK, for example, is released by Sony in the USA. The company in the USA would pay its UK company a royalty on every copy of the album sold, in much the same way as two completely unconnected companies would operate. The main difference would be that the royalty paid would be much higher than that which would be paid by a third-party company, and that there would be no advance.

Under the terms of most licensing arrangements, all manufacturing, marketing and promotional expenses, along with publishing payments, would be paid by the licensee company, as such payments would usually be non-recoupable from either the artist or the licensor. In other words, the licensor would have borne most or all of the original recoupable costs (signing the band, recording the album, making videos and so on) in its home territory, and would now be looking to the royalties flowing in from its overseas licensee as a source of income to assist in recouping these costs.

Occasionally, certain costs borne by the overseas licensee – such as unusual promotional expenses or touring costs – may be agreed as being recoupable by the licensor. Some or all of these costs would inevitably find their way onto the band's debit balance rather than simply being viewed as recoupable between the licensor and licensee.

Many companies have long-term licensing deals with overseas licensees which cover all of the product they release, with an overall advance paid by the licensee in return for all of the licensor's output. Such deals are usually exclusive arrangements, or at least 'first-look' deals, which give the licensee the right of first refusal when the licensor has product to offer.

licensing your product

It may seem far fetched to imagine that a record label in an overseas territory might want to release your product, but this is by no means an unlikely situation, depending on the musical genre in which you produce music. To use a working example, a genre such as death metal is so specific in its target market that a number of specialist labels for this genre exist in all of the major territories of the world. If you have produced a great death metal album, and have enjoyed some great press coverage, won some notoriety (perhaps gained using your web site) and maybe some airplay in that territory, then there will more than likely be labels interested in licensing the rights for that album.

If your music is less genre specific, it will undoubtedly be difficult to licence your product, although not impossible. The reason for this is that you will be approaching labels with a far more general A&R policy, and who will undoubtedly be offered huge amounts of domestic product. In these circumstances, you will be required to concentrate harder on making sure that there is a solid set of reasons why overseas labels should have an interest in selling your music.

All labels will be interested in knowing if there is a story behind the band in their home territory – in other words, has the band made a sufficient impact at home to cause a buzz, generate some great reviews, build up a touring base, and sell some records? It might even be the case that your releases in the UK have had some export sales to the territory in question. If this can be conclusively proved then you are already ahead of the game in terms of generating a possible licensing deal. Conversely, it's naïve to think that you can approach an overseas label with a tape, a photo and a finished album, and expect them to pounce on the opportunity of striking up a deal with you.

As we already seen, anyone can make a record – the music industry may have many problems at the moment, but a shortage of release-hungry artists isn't one of them. In fact, almost the reverse is true.

timing

It's certainly the case that there is little point in approaching overseas licensees until a product has been mastered, manufactured and (ideally) released in the UK. A well-constructed package with a finished album and a clutch of reviews will make you appear much more credible than an advance copy of an album which, in the jaundiced view of the potential licensee, may or may not even be getting a release in its home territory. Even assuming that you managed to have your album released simultaneously in a few territories, this approach can cause logistical and promotional nightmares for even the most efficient major record companies, so it's much better to be realistic and take things in stages.

the product

It's best to be frank and say straight away that the chances of getting a licence deal for a one-off single are extremely slim. The exception to this rule is in that genre loosely categorised as 'dance', where instead the record is usually more marketable than the artist's image. It may be possible to negotiate one-off licence deals (perhaps with the option to handle future product built in) with licensees who may view the dance track in question to be marketable both on 12" and also on compilation albums in their territory, particularly if the single in question has had good radio and press reviews in the UK.

For most other genres, deals will be restricted to full albums or, at a stretch, mini albums. As you would imagine, this is because any licensee will be looking to acquire product that will not only sell for a premium price but also has a chance of attracting serious reviews and selling large numbers on a long-term basis.

the package

Approaching potential licensees requires a methodical and strategic plan. You will need to have not only a great record but also some favourable reviews, an impressive biography and some striking photographs, and perhaps even a promo video. For the purposes of the rest of this chapter, we will assume that the band has reached the following stage in the UK:

- There is an album released, which has been distributed properly throughout the UK

- The album has received favourable reviews, if not in the major music titles then at least in some publications that are well respected and may sell overseas

- The band has an ever-increasing live following, and has received glowing live reviews in the discerning music publications. For example, there may have been a live review in the *NME*, or the band may have been tipped as the next big thing in *Time Out*. (Both of these publications have a good reputation overseas.)

These factors will operate together to help convince a licensee that, if the band is starting to develop a 'story' in the UK, perhaps now would be a good time to jump on board. It's important not to underestimate the influence of the UK media (even in some of the more unlikely corners of the world), or the way in which the Internet is being used to disseminate this information instantaneously. Remember that, only a few short years ago, a small punk label in Tokyo or Chicago would have to wait the best part of a week for their cherished copy of the *NME* to arrive on their doorstep; they can now get *NME* updates daily, and for free.

We will also assume that the band is operating in a musical genre that is fairly specific and has a very easily identifiable demographic, and that there has already been some interest shown in them, however small, from parties outside the UK. This interest could simply be an increase in web site activity, or perhaps some favourable reviews from radio DJs and journalists.

how to find licensees

Discovering the details of the many potential licensees around the world isn't as difficult as you may think, but it will still take some time and dedication to research them, using both traditional media resources and the Internet. The best way to approach this is first to define your genre as brutally and realistically as you can, so that you can then narrow down your target list. Next, try to identify a list of territories in which there seems to be a new or constant interest in your particular genre of music in the press. For example, from reading the popular music press you may have become aware that there is an active and growing metal scene in Scandinavia at present. With the employment of some lateral thinking and from leafing through half a dozen different rock and metal magazines, it's a safe bet that a day on the Internet will probably yield the names and web site addresses of literally dozens of rock labels in Denmark, Norway, Sweden and Finland.

The next stage in the proceedings is to create a database of the appropriate labels, compiling not only details of their addresses, telephone numbers, fax numbers, email addresses and web site locations, but also details of the other bands that are currently on their rosters. You will then need to find out the right person to approach at each label (hopefully the web site may provide you with some clues in this). If you're in any doubt, you should approach the managing director, the head of acquisition or the head of international at each label. A brief and politely-worded email should do the trick, such as something along the lines of the following:

Dear (name of contact)

Re: (name of band)

We represent (name of band), who have just released their debut album in the UK, distributed by (distributor). The album has received excellent reviews (a four-star review in Q magazine) and the band have built up a large following in the UK. We are now looking for overseas licence deals for the album, and have been looking at your web site with interest. More details on the band can be found at their web site, at (address).

We would welcome details of the right person to whom we should send a copy of the album.

Yours sincerely etc.

Again, it creates a much better impression if it it appears that band has a label behind it, and if the distributor which they are using is large or at least well known.

Once a target list of labels has been compiled (by territory), you will need to send off brief letters of introduction with each package, and clearly mark each package with the words "requested material". If you have heard nothing from the label after around three weeks (it may take a package three or four days to reach an address in Europe, even if sent via airmail), don't be afraid to send a gentle reminder by fax or e-mail. If, at the end of the day, the label displays no interest, there may be a chance of your package being returned, if you ask them nicely, which will at least save you some money, and you'll then be able to send the package out to another target.

If you're reluctant to adopt the administratively-intense approach of researching potential licensees yourself, it may be more cost effective for you to consider attending trade fairs or conventions, such as In The City (UK), MIDEM (Cannes, France) or Popkomm (Cologne, Germany). Any industry gathering will contain representatives from a number of labels looking for product to licence, even if the event is primarily focused on the UK music scene and driven largely by A&R, such as In The City.

MIDEM, which takes place in Cannes at the end of January, is still the most significant forum for the investigation and conclusion of licensing deals. The event attracts around 4,000 companies each year, ranging from record labels and publishers to pressing plants and Internet companies, and at least some of them are looking to obtain product licensing deals. Unfortunately, however, the focus tends to be on the sellers rather than the buyers, at least in terms of licensing. MIDEM is an expensive event to attend (registration costs around £400), and unless you're a delegate you won't be allowed to enter the main trade arena at the Palais Des Festivals. That said, however, much of the actual business activity tends to be conducted in the bars and hotels around the main site, rather like the Cannes Film Festival, or at any one of the large number of concerts and showcases that take place.

The MIDEM website (www.midem.com) is a mine of information, and also contains the names and home countries of each year's delegates. Although you have to register with MIDEM to gain access to the full site, with some lateral thinking and plenty of time you may be able to find each company's own site.

It would be unwise to set a great deal of store by such events, but if you happen to be using a UK distributor who is also attending the event it may be possible to ask them to represent your product to potential licensees on an agency basis, in a similar way to that discussed previously. Many bands are tempted to invest a great deal of money to mount expensive showcases at MIDEM and other trade fairs, and this is an approach which may produce favourable results in some circumstances, although perhaps not the one that they might expect. It may transpire that you find yourself enjoying more interest from publishers and concert promoters than that from record labels or Internet companies.

other approaches

There are myriad other approaches which you can take to bring your music to the attention of overseas labels, without taking the formal approach of sending out hundreds of packages.

Liaise with your solicitor to see if he or she can recommend a music attorney in America whom you could approach and hire them to act on your behalf, perhaps one with whom your solicitor deals regularly, or with whom he or she has a particularly good personal relationship. US attorneys tend to be much more pro-active than UK solicitors when it comes to passing on material to those record labels they feel would be interested, potential US managers, or agents.

You could also investigate overseas media opportunities, which could include the possibility of having an import of your album reviewed in local music publications and/or played on influential radio stations in particular territories. With careful research, and with help from your overseas fans via your web site, you should be able to get a good idea of at least some of the opinion formers in the press and on the radio in most of the major territories, and e-mailing them a short message, including a link to your site, may produce dividends. If you can land even a small amount of radio play on some credible stations, the DJ or producer who plays your material may be able to pass on your material to a label, along with a strong recommendation.

If you're able to find some support slots for your band in London or the major cities, and the headline band is from overseas, find out to which home label they're signed. Make sure that you provide the band, their manager or hopefully their label representative (if present) with a package of your material. Bands always listen to other the music of other bands, and if you can forge a relationship with them then the people at their label are more likely to be receptive to your material.

The *Music Week* directory lists certain companies who specialise in finding ex-UK licensing deals (under the 'Business Miscellaneous' section). Although this is pretty much a grey area, there is no doubt that the forging of contacts and networking form a cornerstone of the international music business. Many licensing companies are run by people who used to be senior staff at record companies, and as such have unrivalled contacts within labels all over the world. Although they are much more likely to involve themselves with established artists than with new artists, they may take them under their wings if the band in question has strong story in the UK, particularly if the band is operating in a musical genre in which they specialise. These companies usually operate on a commission basis, taking a percentage of the advance and royalty payable by the licensee, but there are other occasions on which they will insist on licensing overseas rights from you themselves and then sub-licensing these rights to other labels.

If you're in the fortunate position of having signed a publishing deal, however small, then your publisher is likely to have sub-publishing or administration deals in some of the major overseas territories, if not all of them. These contacts should be used pro-actively to develop possible licensing deals, not least because the sub-publisher will benefit from the release of the product in that particular territory.

Compilation CDs are also an effective way of bringing yourself to the attention of potential licensees, and these can be given away as cover mounts on overseas music titles or used by overseas labels and distributors as promotional tools. Although you're unlikely to receive anything in the way of an advance, a fee or a royalty for one of your tracks being included on this kind of release, compilation CDs are still a valuable commodity, and can prove vital in raising the profile of your band. You should ensure that the artwork of such a release will credit your band, and it should also include some kind of notification that you're available for licence, together with your web-site and e-mail addresses.

licensing agreements

If you're successful in attracting interest from an overseas label, the normal sequence of events would be that the label would make you a written offer for the rights, which – if you agreed the terms offered by them – would then be followed up by the issue of a so-called 'Heads Of Agreement'. This is a more detailed document, designed to be signed by both parties and containing all of the basic terms of the agreement without using the long and involved terminology used in a full contract. Such basic terms are often called the 'boilerplate' terms of the agreement.

'Heads Of Agreements' are usually made subject to contract, but in reality there are a number of occasions on which a 'heads of' agreement would be signed and a full-length agreement never formalised. Although this is not the recommended approach, if both parties proceed on the basis of the 'heads of' agreement then there is effectively a binding contract already existing between them.

Of course, you should also consult your solicitor if you receive a formal offer from a licensee, but if you want to save time and money you will need to be looking for the following elements in any offer.

rights

The licensee will wish to be in control of the right to manufacture, sell and distribute your album in their territory, and to allow other companies the right to do so. You should ensure that your licensee doesn't also take the right to sub-licence your product to other companies in their territory, if this isn't what you agreed, because this will undoubtedly reduce the royalty.

Although it's unlikely that any licensee would attempt to obtain download rights in your recordings as part of their deal, you must ensure that the rights which you grant him or her are specifically restricted to sales which take place through retail outlets (record shops) and, in certain circumstances, mail order. The primary grant of rights should also ensure that the licensee is only permitted to release the album in an agreed format, and with agreed artwork, even if this differs from the UK version of the release, and also that he or she is not permitted to release singles from the album or to use tracks on compilation albums, unless this has been agreed specifically.

royalties and advances

There are a number of questions that you should ask before entering into this kind of arrangement. For instance, what is the rate of royalty which is being offered, and on what price is the percentage based? Is there an advance payment offered against this royalty, and, if so, in what instalments is it staged, and how will it be paid?

It would be unusual not to be offered an advance by a licensee, however small, if only as an indication that they are serious in their approach, and that they feel that there will be sufficient sales to give the advance chance to recoup.

If the advance is very low, you may be able to persuade the relevant people at the label to let you have a larger-than-average amount of 'promotional' copies of the release, which you can then sell at your live appearances or through your web site. Remember, however, that if you appear to be importing goods for sale you may attract the attention of HM Customs And Excise, and you will be required to pay VAT.

The remitting of an advance should normally be carried out by direct bank transfer, and you should take into account any bank charges that you are likely to suffer if this method is used. On an advance worth US $1,000, a £40 bank charge for conversion into sterling, coupled with transfer fees, will in fact amounts to a significant percentage of the total.

The value of the Royalty Base Price is normally calculated with either a retail formula or a dealer price formula, and the final amount will be subject to a number of deductions (perhaps for packaging costs, free goods and other areas in which a reduced rate is traditionally implemented, such as sales through record clubs and mail order companies). However, all of these areas will be open to negotiation.

Once the 'Heads Of Agreement' has been signed, on no account should you release master material to a licensee until the agreed first instalment of the advance is in the bank.

territory and term

In which territories are you being asked to grant the licensee rights to release your product, and for how long? From the licensee's point of view, they will be looking to release the album in their home territory and in others in which they have a significant presence, and if they are a European-based licensee then the question is almost irrelevant – they will expect to export product all over the continent. You should be wary of granting rights to the licensee in a territory they will have only a limited chance of achieving sales, because by doing so you will be removing your ability to find an alternative licensee who may sell more product. For example, your lawyer will ensure that a definition of a territory as 'North America' is narrowed down to 'the United States of America' (if you don't intend to grant rights in Canada to the licensee).

The licensee will be looking to be in control of the rights for as long as possible – usually at least five years – in order to exploit the album to the fullest possible extent. It may be possible to build in 'trigger points' during the term so that, for example, the term is only extended from five years if a certain number of sales have been achieved, or recoupment has occurred.

accounting

The agreement will need to be absolutely precise about the accounting periods for which you will receive royalty statements (which, if your advance has been recouped, will hopefully be accompanied by a further payment). It would be usual for such royalty statements to be sent to you every six months, a certain number of days after the end of each calendar half-year (60 days, for example). Such provisions may allow the licensee to take a reserve against possible returns from their distributor or retailer before they remit royalties to the licensor.

other provisions

- You should insist on a release commitment, whereby the licensee guarantees to release the album within a given time frame

- The agreement should include provisions relating to what should occur should either party breach the terms of the agreement, what should be done to rectify this breach, and it should also define the time period during which this action must take place

- There should be a provision included which determines what will happen at the end of the term, regarding the selling of stock by the licensee and the destruction or return of any remaining stock and copy masters.

Of course, these guidelines are no substitute for employing a solicitor to deal with the 'heads of' agreement, but if you already have an understanding of the basic points that are likely to form the bedrock of the deal, it will certainly save you time and money.

licensing in the UK

So far it has been assumed that the band in question are acting as their own record label, distributing, releasing and marketing their own product. However, there are many other hybrid arrangements which could be adopted, which are made possible by virtue of the band having recorded their own product and owning all of the rights in it.

Imagine that you have a fully-recorded and -mastered album, complete with with basic artwork, which you intend to release yourself through the various routes discussed previously (retail distribution, your web site and concert sales). It may be the case that there are a number of small labels which the band have encountered on their journey to this point, who had neither the money or the resources to sign the band even though they may have been interested. It may be the case that they had offered the band a one-off single deal which was rejected, or that the band were unwilling to sign an unfavourable deal with the label.

Now that you're in the driving seat and have an album ready, however, you're in a much stronger position, and it may be possible for you to use such a relationship with a small label to your advantage. Rather than signing to them under a long term deal, you may be able to license your album to them under terms which are enormously favourable to you, to relieve yourself of some of the financial risk and administrative headaches.

For the label, the advantages of such an arrangement are clear: it's being being presented with a finished product, which it can evaluate on its merits, rather than having to sign the band and hope that they can come up with the goods in the studio; it's also in a position where it can limit its financial exposure, particularly if the band are looking for a realistic advance.

For the band, the advantages are that they have already made the album that they wanted to make, and they retain the copyright; they are also in a position to use the label's distribution arrangements, which may be more effective than those which they can find themselves; also, they can use the fact that they have already borne the financial burden of recording to persuade the label to agree to favourable financial terms; and finally, the band won't necessarily be tied to providing the label with product in the future.

Every deal is different, and there area many possible scenarios. If a small but enthusiastic label was desperate to release the album in question, a 'split-profit' arrangement may be possible, by which the label covers the cost of manufacturing, and appears to release the album; then, after the distributor has deducted their percentage (which may, incidentally, be significantly less than the band could have negotiated themselves with the same distributor) and other agreed costs have been deducted (such as advertising), it may be possible for the remaining net income to be split as much as 75:25 in the band's favour. In this way, the label would use its 25% towards the cost of manufacturing, and the band would use its 75% to help repay the costs it has incurred to date.

Although such an approach may appear to run against the underlying sentiment of this book, it's nonetheless deserving of consideration, as in this situation at least the artists are in control of the deal. Such arrangements should certainly be treated with caution, however, and when dealing with very small labels care should be taken to ensure that your band are accounted to properly. For this reason, it may be necessary to insist on direct accounting from the distributor to the band for its share and to the label for its share, and for the band to retain control of the masters, the manufacturing process and the completed product.

It's also worth mentioning that many smaller independent labels operate 'split profit' deals with the bands they sign (often with a 50:50 split), but this is a different kind of arrangement and usually involves the label retaining control of the copyright in the recordings and extracting larger deductions before the 'net' is achieved.

An extremely basic sample licence deal in 'Heads Of Agreement' form can be found in appendix one.

epilogue

If you've managed to plough through this book this far, you'll undoubtedly be thinking: "This all sounds as though it's going to cost me a lot of money". You're right, of course; the more money you can scrape together then the more effectively you can tailor your approach – as long as that you allocate sensible budgets, of course. But you should remember that the object is to make money, and the only way to do this is to create saleable product, in the form of either merchandise or a record release, and to support this by gigging, which itself will eventually become profitable. And if you're not prepared to spend money on your own career, why have you been blithely assuming that a record company will be prepared to do so?

The phrase you are looking for is the time-honoured axiom "you've got to speculate to accumulate". In order to further your career, you have to make an investment in money, time and commitment right now. After all, what's the alternative? The 'industry' (for want of a better word), in the manifestation of a local promoter or a major record company, will always respect artists who knuckle down and concentrate on building their own careers without waiting for others to do the job for them.

The opportunities offered by the Internet, in enabling both new and established artists to forge direct links with their audiences, will radically change the entire music business. Nobody can predict with any degree of accuracy exactly how many major record companies will exist in a decade, or indeed how the global audience will prefer to their music delivered. The only certainty is that there will always be musicians making great music that deserves to be heard. If you're one of those musicians, take steps now to get your music out there. If you have a great record in you, now is the time to make it.

Don't rely on the music industry to bring your audience to you – go out and find them yourself. And good luck!

sample licensing agreement

The sample agreement below, between a licensor and licensee in respect of an album, is in the form of a 'heads of' agreement, containing all of the main terms that would be included in a full-length agreement. It isn't a substitute for an agreement drafted by, or negotiated by, a specialist music industry solicitor, but will at least give you an idea of what to look out for if you're getting some interest from potential licensees.

THIS AGREEMENT is made the .... (day) of .... (month) .... (year) **BETWEEN** (Licensor's name and address) and (Licensee's name and address), **WHEREAS** Licensor is the owner of the copyright and all other ancillary rights in various sound recordings by (name of band) (the Artists); and Licensee is a record company that wishes to distribute Records featuring such recordings.

NOW IT IS HEREBY AGREED AS FOLLOWS:

1. *Definitions*

   "The Album"

   shall mean the album entitled (name of album) by the Artists embodying the Recordings previously released by the Licensor in the United Kingdom.

   "Recordings"

   shall mean those recordings by (name of band) embodied on the Album previously released in the United Kingdom by the Licensor.

"Artwork"

shall mean the film or computer artwork for the Album owned and controlled by the Licensor, which the Licensor shall send to the Licensee for the purpose of the Licensee making duplicates therefrom.

"Records"

shall mean Compact Discs, Cassettes and Vinyl Records, as those terms are commonly understood in the recording industry.

"Term"

shall mean 3 (three) years commencing on (date).

"Territory"

shall mean Germany, Austria and Switzerland.

"Royalty"

shall mean 18% (eighteen per cent) of the published price to dealers of Records sold and not returned hereunder, which shall be payable by the Licensee to the Licensor upon the Accounting Dates, subject to the recoupment of the Advance.

"Advance"

shall mean the sum of DM 10,000 (ten thousand deutschmarks), which shall be a recoupable but non-returnable payment against the Royalty, and payable by the Licensee to the Licensor upon the signature hereof by direct bank transfer.

"Accounting Dates"

shall mean 90 days from the end of June and December in each year of the Term.

2.   *Grant Of Rights*

The Licensor hereby grants to the Licensee the sole and exclusive right in the Territory during the Term to manufacture, sell and distribute Records comprising only the Recordings in the format of the Album, and to cause third parties to do so on the Licensee's behalf, in consideration of the payment by the Licensee to the Licensor of the Royalty and the Advance.

The Licensee undertakes to release the album in the Territory by no later than (date).

3. *Manufacture And Artwork*

The Licensee shall be permitted to adapt the Artwork to a design over which the Licensor shall have sole approval, but which shall incorporate the Licensee's catalogue number and logo, as well as the Licensor's logo. The following requirements also must be incorporated into any such new artwork:

i)   All lyrics of the Recordings and all credits appearing on the Artwork;

ii) A copyright line to the effect that the copyright in the sound recordings is owned by the Licensor, under exclusive licence to the Licensee for the Territories of Germany, Austria and Switzerland;

iii) Contact details for (name of band) Management, Information Service and Web Site.

The Licensor shall supply to the Licensee further photographs of the Artist in order that Licensee may create such adapted artwork.

In the final 6 (six) months of the Term, the Licensee shall not manufacture copies of the Album in quantities in excess of those sold in the previous 6 (six) months of the Term.

4. *Accounting*

The Licensee shall account to the Licensor on the Accounting Dates in respect of the Royalty due on sales of the Album, and shall give detailed statements concerning the number of Records of the Album sold in each part of the Territory to Licensor, the published price of such sales to dealers, and the amount of Royalty due. In the event that such statement(s) show that that Advance has been recouped, the Licensee shall remit payment to the Licensor of monies due with such statement(s).

5. *Promotion*

The Licensor shall ensure that the Artists undertake reasonable promotional and press duties relating to the release of the Album, provided that the Licensee funds any and all expenses connected therewith, and provided that such press and promotional commitments are scheduled with regard to other personal and business commitments of the Artists.

The Licensor shall also ensure that the Artists will consider any reasonable touring engagements in the Territory, provided that the Licensee acknowledges that the cost of such touring engagements must be covered, including profit, from tour fees payable to the Artists.

The Licensee undertakes to promote the release of the Album in the Territory by way of a reasonable marketing and promotional spending on press advertising and in-store promotion, together with radio promotion.

6. *Publishing*

The Licensee shall be entirely and solely responsible for meeting the cost of the publishing payments due in respect of the manufacture and sale of Records of the Album in the Territory at standard industry rates, and for completing any and all necessary licences and other documentation relating to mechanical royalty payments in the Territory.

7. *Breach*

In the event that the Licensee is in material breach of its obligations hereunder and has not remedied such breach within 30 (thirty) days of the Licensor notifying the Licensee thereof, then the Licensor shall be entitled to terminate this agreement forthwith and require the Licensee to cease its distribution and sale of the Album in the Territory.

8. *Miscellaneous*

i) **Single Release**

In the event that the Licensee wishes to release a so-called Single Record comprising two or more of the Recordings in the Territory, then – provided that the royalty payable in respect of such release is equal to the Royalty – the Licensor grants consent, in principle, to such a release, subject to approval of artwork and promotional plans for such a release.

ii) **Compilation Albums**

The Licensor does not grant to the Licensee the right to license to third parties any of the Recordings or the Additional Recordings for inclusion on compilation albums, or for the Licensee itself to release the Recordings or Additional Recordings on such compilation albums, without the prior written consent of the Licensor.

iii) Sample Copies

The Licensee undertakes to supply to the Licensor with 100 (one hundred) sample copies of the Licensee version of the Album upon the release of the Album, at no cost to Licensor.

iv) Expiry Of Term

Upon the expiry of the Term, the Licensee's rights hereunder shall end and the Licensee shall offer the Licensor the opportunity to purchase any unsold stock of the Album at manufacturing cost. If the Licensor does not elect to purchase any or all of such stock then the Licensee shall destroy such stock and provide the Licensor with a certificate of the destruction thereof.

v) Applicable Law

This agreement shall be governed by the laws of England and Wales. Nothing herein shall be deemed to constitute a partnership or joint venture between the parties hereto.

IN WITNESS WHEREOF THE PARTIES HERETO HAVE SET THEIR HAND

Signed ....Date ....
an authorised signatory for the Licensor

Witnessed ....

Signed ....Date ....
an authorised signatory for the Licensee

Witnessed ....

London rehearsal rooms

Backstreet

313 Holloway Road, London N7 9SU
Tel: (020) 7609 1313
Fax: (020) 7609 5229
Email: backstreetstudios@virgin.net

John Henry Enterprises

16-24 Brewery Road
Tel: (020) 7609 9181
Fax: (020) 7700 7040
Email: andreaw@johnhnrys.com

La Rocka Studios

Postmark House, Cross Lane, London N8 7SA
Tel: (020) 8348 2822
Fax: (020) 8347 5390

Mega City One

24-28 Hatton Wall, London EC1
Tel: (020) 7419 9455

Nomis Studios

45-53 Sinclair Road, London W14 0NS
Tel: (020) 7602 6351
Fax: (020) 7300 6515
Email: rehearsals@nomisstudios.co.uk

Panic Studios

Unit 15, 19 Victoria Road, London NW10 6NB
Tel: (020) 8961 9540
Fax: (020) 8838 2194

Survival Studios

Unit B18 Acton Business Centre, School Road, North Acton, London NW10
Tel: (020) 8961 1977

Terminal Studios

4-10 Lamb Walk, London Bridge, London SE1 3TT
Tel: (020) 7403 3050
Fax: 7407 6123
Email: rehearsal@terminal.co.uk

Waterloo Sunset

Top Floor, Buildings C And D, Tower Bridge Business Centre, 100
Clements Road, London SE16 4DG
Tel: (020) 7252 0001

Westar Studios

4-6 Priory Way, Southall, Middlesex UB2 5EH
Tel: (020) 8571 4679
Email: westarstudios@cwcom.net

regional rehearsal rooms

Berkeley 2

54 Washington Street, Glasgow G3 8AZ
Tel: 0141 248 7290
Fax: 0141 204 1138

Crash Rehearsal Rooms

Imperial Warehouse, 11 Davies Street, Liverpool, Merseyside L1 6HB
Tel: 0151 236 0989
Fax 0151 236 0989

Epic Head Studios

PO Box 183, Sheffield S1 2XF
Tel: 0114 273 1398
Email: ehead@jadestne.demon.co.uk

Mad Dog Rehearsal

Unit 57 Deeside Industrial Estate, Deeside, Clwyd CH5 2LR
Tel: 01224 281705

House Of Mook

Authorpe Road, Leeds, West Yorkshire LS6 4JB
Tel: 0113 230 4008

Noisebox

135-137 King Street, Mountergate, Norwich, Norfolk NR1 1QH
Tel: 01603 767726
Fax: 01603 767746
Email: info@noisebox.co.uk

One Groove

Clifton Works, 76 John Street, Sheffield S2 4QU
Tel: 0114 279 5650

QTEN Studio

Unit Q-10, Queensway Industrial Estate, Glenrothes, Fife KY7 5PZ
Tel: 01592 611327
Fax: 01592 610315
Email: icobra@fife.ac.uk

Renaissance Studios

Olympic House, Middlewood Street, Salford, Manchester M5 1RF
Tel: 0161 835 1916

Rich Bitch Rehearsals

505 Bristol Road, Selly Oak, Birmingham B29 6AU
Tel: 0121 471 1339

Soundstation

37 Commercial Street, Birmingham B1 1RS
Tel: 0121 643 5952

Unit 3 Rehearsal Studios

Unit 3 St Catherine's Industrial Estate, Whitehouse Lane, Bedminster,
Bristol BS3
Tel: 0117 949 3323

Warehouse Studios

60 Sandford Lane, Kennington, Oxford OX1 5RW
Tel: 01865 736411

regional club venues

The Adelphi

89 De Grey Street, Hull
Tel: 01482 348216

The Attic

Upstart Productions, The Ark, 3 Semple Street, Edinburgh EH3 8BL
Tel: 0131 220 2797

Band On The Wall

25 Swan Street, Manchester M4 5JQ
Tel: 0161 832 6625

The Boat Race

Tel: 01223 508 533
170 East Road, Cambridge CB1 1DB

The Brook

466 Portswood Road, Southampton SO17 3AN
Tel: 01703 555366
Fax: 01703 341001

The Cavern Club

83-84 Queen Street, Exeter, Devon EX4 3RP
Tel: 01392 495 370
Fax: 01392 271 625
Email: exetercavern@hotmail.com

Clwb I For Bach

Wombany Street, Cardiff
Tel: 01223 503 508533

The Concorde

57 Marine Drive, Brighton, East Sussex BN2 7HQ
Fax: 01273 309 91

Fibbers

Units 8-12 Stonebow House, Stonebow, York, North Yorkshire Y01 7NP
Tel: 01904 651250
Fax: 07070 716747
Email: fibbers@btinternet.com
Website: www.fibbers.co.uk

The Foundry

Beak Street, Birmingham, West Midlands B1 1LS
Tel: 0121 622 1894

The Leadmill

6-7 Leadmill Road, Sheffield S1 4SE
Tel: 0114 275 4500
Fax: 0114 221 2848
Email: promotions@leadmiltd.freeserve.co.uk

The Lemon Tree

5 West North Street, Aberdeen AB24 5AT
Tel: 01224 647 99
Fax: 01224 630888

The Louisiana

Wapping Road, Bristol
Tel: 0117 926 5978

The Lomax

34 Cumberland Street, Liverpool L1 6BU
Tel: 0151 707 9977

The Point

The Plain, Oxford OX4 1EA
Tel: 01865 798 794

The Portland Arms (Cambridge)

Tel: 01223 565 366

The Roadhouse (Manchester)

Tel: 0161 237 9789

The Robin Hood

Merry Hill, Brierley Hill, West Midlands DY5 1TD
Tel: 01384 637747
Fax: 01384 637227

The Robin Hood 2

Mount Pleasant, Bilston, Wolverhampton, West Midlands WV14 7LJ
Tel: 01384 637747
Fax: 01384 637227

The Varsity (Wolverhampton)

Tel: 01902 711166

The Wedgewood Rooms (Portsmouth)

Tel: 01705 863 911

London club venues

The Barfly Club

234 Royal College Street, London NW1 9LT
Tel: (020) 7482 4808
Fax: (020) 7482 4809
Email: barfly@avnet.co.uk

The Borderline

Orange Yard, Manette Street, Charing Cross, London W1V 6JB
Tel: (020) 7287 1441
Fax: (020) 7434 1698
Email: daisyjac@hotmail.com

The Bull And Gate

389 Kentish Town Road, London NW5 2TJ
Tel: (020) 7485 5358
Fax: (020) 7689 0743
Email: info@bullandgate.co.uk

Dingwalls

Middle Yard, Camden, London NW1
Tel: (020) 7267 1577

The Dublin Castle

94 Parkway, Camden, London NW1
Tel: (020) 7378 6095
Fax: (020) 7378 6104
Email: info@bugbear18.freeserve.co.uk

The Electric Ballroom

184 Camden High Street, London NW1 8QP

Tel: (020) 7485 9006
Fax: (020) 7284 0745

The Garage

20-22 Highbury Corner, London N5 1RD
Tel: (020) 8961 5490
Fax: (020) 8961 9238

The Half Moon

93 Lower Richmond Road, London SW5 1EU
Tel: (020) 8780 9383
Fax: (020) 8789 7863
Email: carrie@halfmoon.co.uk

The Hope And Anchor

207 Upper Street, London N1 1BZ
Tel: (020) 7378 6095
Fax: (020) 7378 6104
Email: info@bugbear.freeserve.co.uk

The Jazz Café

5 Parkway, London NW1
Tel: (020) 7916 6060
Fax: (020) 7916 6622
Email: adrian@jazzcafe.demon.co.uk

LA2

165 Charing Cross Road, London WC2H 0EN
Tel: (020) 7434 9592
Fax: (020) 7437 1781

The Mean Fiddler

24-28A High Street, Harlesden, London NW10 4LX
Tel: (020) 8961 5490
Fax: (020) 8961 2338
Email: astoria@freeserve.co.uk

The Monarch

49 Chalk Farm Road, Camden, London NW1 8AN
Tel: (020) 7916 1049
Fax: (020) 7209 2479
Email: tiffar@aol.com

The 100 Club

100 Oxford Street, London W1N 9FB
Tel: (020) 7636 0933
Fax: (020) 7436 1958

The Orange

3 North End Crescent, North End Road, London W14 8TG
Tel: (020) 7381 0444
Fax: (020) 7381 0281

The Rock Garden

6-7 The Piazza, Covent Garden, London WC2E 8HA
Tel: (020) 7836 4052
Fax: (0282) 7379 4793

Water Rats Theatre

328 Grays Inn Road, London WC1X 8BZ
Tel: (020) 7580 8881
Fax: (020) 7580 8882
Email: backyard@bogo.co.uk

The Scala

Pentonville Road, London N1
Tel: (020) 7833 2022

Subterrania

12 Acklam Road, London W10 5QZ
Tel: (020) 8961 5490
Fax: (020) 8961 9238

artwork designers

Ara Art

138A Chiswick High Road, London W4 1PU
Tel: (020) 8994 9007
Fax: (020) 8995 1051
Email: jiggy@hiphop.com

Bassline Design

67-69 Whitfield Street, London W1P 5RL
Tel: (020) 7468 3669
Fax: (020) 7255 2131

Carrera Design

Elwy Valley Studios, Tan-y-Clogwyn, Llangernyw LL22 8RH
Tel: 01745 860 652
Fax: 01745 860 485
Email: design@carrerarecordings.com

Colors

42-44 Hanway Street, London W1P 9DE
Tel: (020) 7637 1842
Fax: (020) 7637 5568
Email: colors@colors.co.uk

DS Advertising Design Ltd

Chantry House, Victoria, Leeds, West Yorkshire LS5 3JB
Tel: 0113 225 7100
Fax: 0113 225 7200
Email: Matt@dsad.co.uk

Fluid

Studio 1/222, The Custard Factory, Gibb Street, Birmingham, West
Midlands B9 4AA
Tel: 0121 693 6913
Fax 0121 693 6911
Email: drop@fluidesign.co.uk

David Larkham Design

41 Great Windmill Street, London W1V 7PA
Tel: (020) 7437 7206
Fax: (020) 7434 3884

Mental Block

165 Battersea Rise, London SW11 1HP
Tel: (020) 7924 2217
Fax: (020) 7924 2117
Email: sales@mentalblock.co.uk

Orange Curve

46 Cray Road, Sidcup, Kent DA14 4BZ
Tel: (020) 8308 1564
Fax: (020) 8300 3477
Email: design@orangecurve.co.uk

Printout

Rock House, Wheatsheaf Corner, Shiney Row, Tyne And Wear
DH4 4QX
Tel: 0191 385 6591
Fax: 0191 385 6616

Shoot That Tiger!

69 Rivington Street, London EC2A 3AY
Tel: (020) 7613 3599
Fax: (020) 7613 3088
Email: shootthattiger@btinternet.com

Think Tank

Unit 1, The Stable Yard, 16a Balham Hill London SW12 9EB
Tel: (020) 8673 2525
Fax: (020) 8673 2625
Email: info@tsoftnet.co.uk

Zip Design

Unit 2A Queens Studios, 121 Salisbury Road, London
NW6 6RG

Tel: (020) 7372 4474
Fax: (020) 7372 4484
Email: info@zipdesign.demon.co.uk

manufacturers and duplicators

A To Z Music Services

43-51 Wembley Hill Road, Wembley, Middlesex HA9 8AU
Tel: (020) 8903 0046
Fax: (020) 8782 4601
Email: info@a2zmusic.co.uk

AWL Compact Disc Company

356 Scaptoft Lane, Leicester LE5 1PB
Tel: 0116 241 3979
Fax: 0116 243 3760

CD Plant

29-31 Fairview Industrial Estate, Clayton Road, Hayes, Middlesex UB3 1AN
Tel: (020) 8581 9200
Fax: (020) 8581 9249
Email: sales@cdplant.co.uk

Chop Em Out Mastering

Trinity Mews, Cambridge Gardens, London
Tel: (020) 8960 8128
Fax: (020) 8968 0341
Web site: www.chopemout.com

DOCdata

50 York Road, Battersea, London SW11 3SJ
Tel: (020) 7801 2400
Fax: (020) 7801 0945
Email: admin@docdata.demon.co.uk

Forward Sound And Vision (Vinyl)

Sterling Industrial Estate, Rainham Road South, Dagenham, Essex
RM10 8HP
Tel: (020) 8592 0242
Fax: (020) 8595 8182
Web site: www.fsv.co.uk

Hilton Grove

Hilton Grove Business Centre, Hatherley Mews, Walthamstow, London
E17 4QP
Tel: (020) 8521 2424
Fax: (020) 8521 4343
Email: info@hgrove.demon.co.uk

Ital Supply

Suite 3, 424 Seven Sisters Road, London N4 2LX
Tel: (020) 8880 1302
Fax: (020) 8800 7750
Email: italsupply@hotmail.com

Key Production

2 Hargrave Place, London N7 0BP
Tel: (020) 7485 7499
Fax: (020) 7284 1151

Offside Manufacturing

Ground Floor, Unit 9, Blenheim Court, 62 Brewery Road, London N7 9NY
Tel: (020) 7700 2662
Fax: (020) 7700 2882
Email: richard@backstreet-intl.com

Repeat Performance Mastering

6 Grand Union Centre, West Row, London W10 5AS
Tel: (020) 8960 7222
Fax: (020) 8968 1378
Web site: www.repeatperformance.co.uk

RTS Onestop

Unit M2, Albany Road, Prescot, Merseyside L34 2SH
Tel: 0151 430 9001
Fax: 0151 430 7441
Email: rts.Onestop@virgin.net

Sounds Good

12 Chiltern Enterprise Centre, Station Road, Theale, Berkshire RG7 4AA

Tel: 0118 930 1700
Fax: 0118 930 1709
Web site: www.sounds-good.co.uk

Sound Performance

80 Blackheath Road, London SE10 8DA
Tel: (020) 8691 2121
Fax: (020) 8691 3144
Email: sales@soundperformance.co.uk

Spool Multi Media

Unit 30, Deeside Industrial Park, Deeside, Flintshire CH5 2NU
Tel: 01244 280 602
Fax: 01244 288 581
Email: admin@smmuk.demon.co.uk

merchandising companies

Active Merchandise

Unit 28, The Old Silk Mill, Brook Street, Tring, Hertfordshire HP23 5EF
Tel: 01442 827 403
Fax: 01442 827400
Email: active@rotator.co.uk

Backstreet International Merchandise

Unit 9, Blenheim Court, 62 Brewery Road, London N7 9NY
Tel: (020) 7700 2662
Fax: (020) 7700 2882
Email: andy@backstreet-intl.com

Brilliant Merchandising

PO Box 905, London SE1 6LF
Email: brilliant@dial.pipex.com

The Cap Company

The Old Dispensary, 36 The Millfields, Stonehouse, Plymouth, Devon
PL1 3JB
Tel: 01752 267902
Fax: 01752 255663
Email: sales@the-cap-company.co.uk

Fezborough Ltd

Manor Farm Studio, Clevely, Oxfordshire OX7 4DY
Tel: 01608 677 100
Fax: 01608 677 101
Email: kellogs@fezbro.com

Fifth Column

276 Kentish Town Road, London NW5 2AA
Tel: (020) 7485 8599
Fax: (020) 7267 3718

Green Island Promotional Merchandising

15 Freeland Road, London W5 8HR
Tel: (020) 8896 1746
Fax: (020) 8896 1234
Email: greenisland@btinternet.com

Impact Merchandising

PO Box 12774, London SE1 2PH
Tel: (020) 7378 0609
Fax: (020) 7378 9559
Email: mark@impact.DNA-is.com

Leisure Merchandising

Amsua House, 717A North Circular Road, London NW2A 7AH
Tel: (020) 8357 7997
Fax: (020) 8357 7998

Metro Merchandising Ltd

The Warehouse, 60 Queen Street, Desborough, Northhamptonshire
NN14 2RE
Tel: 01536 763100
Fax: 01536 763200
Email: mailbox@metro-ltd.co.uk

Razamataz

4 Derby Street, Colne, Lancashire BB8 9AA
Tel: 01282 861099
Fax: 01282 861327
Email: sales@razamataz.co.uk

Rock-It! Promotions

Unit 1, Altona Buildings, 6 East Grove, Rushden, Northamptonshire
NN10 0AP
Tel: 01933 311179
Fax: 01933 413 413279
Email: rock-it@easynet.co.uk

RTG Branded Apparel

The Old Dispensary, 36 The Millfields, Stonehouse, Plymouth, Devon
PL1 3JB

Tel: 01752 25388
Fax 01752 255663
Email: sales@rtg.co.uk

Tradewinds Merchandising

50-56 Wharf Road, London N1 7SF
Tel: (020) 7253 4138
Fax: (020) 7251 4845
Email: tradewinds@easynet.co.uk

Zephyr Flags And Banners

Midland Road, Thrapston, Northamptonshire NN14 4LX
Tel: 01832 734484
Fax: 01832 733064
Email: sskey@zephyrflags.com

web site designers

AMX

7 Soho Square, London W1V 5DD
Tel: (020) 7613 5333
Fax: (020) 7613 5333
Email: jack@amxstudios.com

DC Creative

11A Pratt Mews, London NW1 0AD
Tel: (020) 7387 6854
Fax: (020) 7387 6856
Email: info@dc-creative.co.uk

Design Works

72-76 Newgate Lane, Mansfield, Nottinghamshire NG18 2LQ
Tel: 01623 636636
Fax: 01623 623 360
Email: us@designworks.co.uk

D2 Design

18E Hillgate Place, London SW12 9ER
Tel: (020) 8673 9379
Fax: (020) 8675 8562
Email: d2design@d2design.co.uk

Eyetoeye.com

9 Bradbrook House, Studio Place, London SW1X 8EL
Tel: (020) 7235 8345
Fax: (020) 7235 8345
Email: info@eyetoeye.com

FTG Website Design

163 Upper Richmond Road, Twickenham, London TW1 3AT
Tel: 07970 798620
Fax: 07970 087145
Email: andrew@ftg.co.uk

JML Web Designs

Tel: 0498 786786
Fax: (020) 8906 8684
Email: jonnyl@bogo.co.uk

KMO

Unit 7, 39 Ivanhoe Road, Liverpool, Merseyside L17 8XF
Tel: 0151 727 5628
Fax: 0151 727 5628
Email: kmo@zen.co.uk

Perfect World Programs

Unit 601, 50 Westminster Bridge Road, London SE1 7QY
Tel: (020) 7721 8727
Fax: (020) 7721 8728
Email: enq@perfect-world.co.uk

Pinnacle Internet Services

Electron House, Cray Avenue, St Mary Cray, Orpington, Kent BR5 3JR
Tel: 01689 870622
Fax: 01689 878 269
Email: info.pncl.co.uk

Poptel Internet Services

Tel: 0800 458 9465
Fax: (02) 7254 1102
Email: info@poptel.net

Solaris

111 The Business Design Centre, 52 Upper Street, London N1 0QH
Tel: (020) 7288 6048
Fax: (020) 7288 6047
Email: solaris@donut.demon.co.uk

Springboard Internet Services

La Lumière, 1 Virginia Street, London E1 9BD
Tel: (020) 7782 4700
Fax: (020) 7782 4840

Email: commercial@lineone.net

State 51

91 Brick Lane, London E1 6QN
Tel: (020) 7377 6294
Fax: (020) 7377 6297
Email: intouch@state51.co.uk

useful web sites

Brandnewmusic

Web site: www.brandnewmusic.com
A site devoted to exposing new music as well as reviews on the live music scene.

Channelfly.com

Web site: www.channelfly.com
Site allied to The Barfly organisation and The Fly magazine, promoting club gigs and indie music throughout the UK.

Dotmusic

Web site: www.dotmusic.com
Provides up-to-the-minute news, reviews and information on UK music, with the emphasis on charts and some industry gossip.

Farmclub.com

Web site: www.farmclub.com
Unsigned bands site run by Universal Music, aiming to find new talent and offer them record deals.

Gig Guide UK

Web site: www.gigguide.co.uk
Information on the Scottish live scene.

Independent Underground Music Archive

Web site: www.iuma.com
Database of thousands of unsigned and indie-label musicians.

Intermusic

Web site: www.intermusic.com

Resources for musicians.

Lyrics Server

Web site: www.lyrics.ch
Massive lyrics database to fall back on when you're lacking inspiration!

Making Music

Web site: www.makingmusic.co.uk
Well-thought-out online version of the popular free music magazine.

MPReal

Web site: www.mpreal.com
Another site promoting unsigned bands, currently offering a high income split in bands' favour.

Musicians Union

Web site: www.musiciansunion.org
Official site for the Musicians Union.

NME

Web site: www.nme.com
Online version of the indie weekly.

Peoplesound.com

Web site: www.peoplesound.com
A site devoted to promoting new music through MP3s and CD sales. Publishes a weekly chart in the music press.

Popwire.com

Web site: www.popwire.com
Another unsigned band site designed to promote new music, but taking certain publishing rights in the process.

Ultimate Band List

Web site: www.ubl.com
All-encompassing music directory.

Unsigned Music

Web site: www.unsignedmusic.com
Yet another site promoting unsigned music.

Vitaminic

Web site: www.vitaminic.com

Offers and promotion for new bands. Through a non-exclusive contract, the site sells music by unsigned new artists.

music industry accountants

Arram Berlyn Gardner

Holborn Hall, 100 Grays Inn Road, London WC1X 8BY
Tel: (020) 7400 6000
Fax: (020) 7400 6013
Email: abg@abggroup.co.uk

Baker Tilly

2 Bloomsbury Street, London WC1 3ST
Tel: (020) 7413 5100
Fax: (020) 7413 5101

Bevis And Co

The Coach House, Farm Lane, Ashstead, Surrey KT21 1LU
Tel: 01372 271701
Fax: 01372 271702
Email: cjbevis@compuserve.com

Brown Mcleod

51 Clarkegrove Road, Sheffield, South Yorkshire S10 2NH
Tel: 0114 268 5665
Fax: 0114 268 4161
Email: entsuk@aol.com

Carnmores Royalties Consultants

Lilly House, Fifth Floor, 13 Hanover Square, London W1R 0HW
Tel: (020) 7499 3373
Fax: (020) 7495 7722
Email: carnmores@aol.com

Deloitte & Touche

Hill House, 1 Little New Street
Tel: (020) 7303 3858
Fax: (020) 7936 3000
Email: charles.bradbrook@deloitte.co.uk

EMTACS

61 Loughbrough Road, West Bridgford, Nottingham NG2 7LA
Tel: 0115 981 5001
Fax: 0115 981 5005
Email: emtacs@aol.com

Financial Management

35 Britannia Row, London N1 8QH
Tel: (020) 7226 3377
Fax: (020) 7354 4966

HW Fisher And Company

Acre House, 11-15 William Road, London NW1 3ER
Tel: (020) 7388 7000
Fax: (020) 7380 4900
Email: info@hwfisher.co.uk

Martin Greene Ravden

55 Loudoun Road, London NW8 0DL
Tel: (020) 7625 4545
Fax: (020) 7625 5265
Email: mgr@mgr.co.uk

Nyman Libson Paul

Regina House, 124 Finchley Road, London NW3 5JS
Tel: (020) 7794 5611
Fax: (020) 7431 1109
Email: mail@nymanlibsonpaul.co.uk

The Royalty Compliance Organisation

73 Wimpole Street, London W1M 8DD
Tel: (020) 7487 3281
Fax: (020) 7224 0446
Email: ask@therco.co.uk

Saffery Champness

Fairfax House, Fulwood Place, Grays Inn, London WC1V 6UB
Tel: (020) 7405 2828
Fax: (020) 7405 7887

Email: nkelsey@saffery.com

Ivan Sopher & Co

5 Elstree Gate, Elstree Way, Borehamwood, Hertfordshire WD6 1JD
Tel: (020) 8207 0602
Fax: (020) 8207 6758

Spicer & Co

19 Main Street, Blackrock, Co Dublin, Ireland
Tel: 00 353 1 283 6233
Fax: 00 353 1 283 6229
Email: audit@spicer.ie

Westbury Music Consultants

72 Marylebone Lane, London W1M 5FF
Tel: (020) 7487 5044
Fax: (020) 7935 2270

CC Young & Co

150 Regent Street, London W1R 5FA
Tel: (020) 7432 0337
Fax: (020) 7432 0338

music industry solicitors

Alistair Nicholas Music And Entertainment Law

89A Leathwaite Road, London SW11 6RN
Tel: (020) 7924 1904
Fax: (020) 7783 1764
Email: anicholas@music-room.com

Babbington Bray

70-71 New Bond Street, London W1Y 9DE
Tel: (020) 7493 8840
Fax: (020) 7493 8841
Email: bbandk.com

Bird & Bird

90 Fetter Lane, London EC4A 1JP
Tel: (020) 7415 6000
Fax: (020) 7415 6111
Email: mark.hafke@twobirds.com

Cats Eye Music Consultant

Maple Farm, 56 High Street, Harrold, Bedford
MK43 7DA
Tel: 01234 720785
Fax: 01234 720664
Email: catseye@maplefarm.demon.co.uk

Clintons

55 Drury Lane, London WC2 5SQ
Tel: (020) 7379 60 80
Fax: (020) 7240 9310
Email: info@clintons.co.uk

David Wineman Solicitors

Craven House, 121 Kingsway, London WC2B 6NX
Tel: (020) 7400 7800
Fax: (020) 74007890
Email: law@davidwineman.co.uk

JP Iliesco De Grimaldi

6 Charles Street, London W1X 7 HB
Tel: (020) 7930 5360
Fax: (020) 7629 0958

Dean Marsh & Co

20 Bowling Green Lane, London EC1R 0BD
Tel: (020) 7553 4400
Fax: (020) 7253 8186
Email: info@deanmarsh.com

Gentle Jayes

26 Grosvenor Street, London W1X 0BD
Tel: (020) 7629 3304
Fax: (020) 7493 0246
Email: davidgentle@gentlejayes.com

Howell Jones And Partners

19A Wimbledon Bridge, London SW19 7NH
Tel: (020) 8947 7991
Fax: (020) 8947 8725
Email: scottlaw@btinternet.com

Manches & Co

Aldwych House, 81 Aldwych, London WC2B 4RP
Tel: (020) 7404 4433
Fax: (020) 7430 1133
Email: manchesmedia@manches.co.uk

Rohan & Co

9 Carnaby Street, London W1V 1 PG
Tel: (020) 7439 3089
Fax: (020) 7437 3852

Seddons Solicitors

5 Portman Square, London W1H 0NT
Tel: (020) 7486 9681
Fax: (020) 7935 5049

Email: davidk@seddons.co.uk

Tarlo Lyons Solicitors

Watchmaker Court, 33 St John's Lane, London EC1M 4DB
Tel: (020) 7405 2000
Fax: (020) 7814 9421
Email: info@tarlo-lyons.com

Teacher Stern Selby

37-41 Bedford Row, London WC1R 4JH
Tel: (020) 7242 3191
Fax: (020) 7405 2964
Email: gd@tsslaw.co.uk

Tods Murray WS

66 Queen Street, Edinburgh, Lothian EH2 4NE
Tel: 0131 226 4771
Fax: 0131 624 7170
Email: Richard.Findlay@todsmurray.co.uk

Wolsey & Co

43 St John Street, London EC1 4AN
Tel: (020) 7490 5444
Fax: (020) 7490 5449

music industry organisations

Arts Council of England

14 Great Peter Street, London SW1P 3NQ
Tel: (020) 7333 0100
Fax: (020) 7973 6590
Email: graeme.wall@artscouncil.org.uk

ASCAP (American Society Of Composers, Authors And Publishers)

8 Cork Street, London W1X 1PB
Tel: (020) 7439 0909
Fax: (020) 7434 0073

Band Register

Oxford Music Central, 2nd Floor, 65 George Street, Oxford OX1 2BE
Tel: 01865 798795
Fax: 01865 798796
Email: nbr@bandreg.com

BMI (Broadcast Music Incorporated)

Harley House, Marylebone Road, London NW1 5HN
Tel: (020) 7486 2036
Fax: (020) 7224 1046
Email: bmi.com

BPI (British Phonographic Industry)

25 Savile Row, London W1X 1AA
Tel: (020) 7287 4422
Fax: (020) 7851 4010
Email: general@bpi.co.uk

Guild Of International Songwriters And Composers

Sovereign House, 12 Trewartha Road, Praa Sands, Penzance, Cornwall
TR20 9ST
Tel: 01736 762826
Fax: 01736 763328
Email: songmag@aol.com

IMF (International Managers Forum)

1 Glenthorne Mews, 115a Glenthorne Road, London W6 0LJ
Tel: (020) 8741 2555
Fax: (020) 8741 4856
Email: office@imf-uk.org

ISA (International Songwriters Association)

PO Box 46, Limerick City, Limerick, Ireland
Tel: 00 353 61 228837
Fax: 00 353 61 229464
Email: jliddane@songwriter.iol.ie

MCPS (Mechanical Copyright Protection Society Ltd)

Copyright House, 29-33 Berners Street, London W1P 4AA
Tel: (020) 7580 5544
Fax: (020) 7306 4050
Email: info@mcps.co.uk

MOBO (Music Of Black Origin)

22 Stephenson Way, London NW1 2HD
Tel: (020) 225 5662
Fax: (020) 232 9662
Email: mobo@biggroup.demon.co.uk

Musicians Union

60-62 Clapham Road, London SW9 0JJ
Tel: (020) 7582 5566
Fax: (020) 7582 9805
Email: musiciansunion.org.uk

National Union Of Student Entertainments

45 Underwood Street, London N1 7LG
Tel: (020) 7490 0946
Fax: (020) 7490 1026
Email: waves@mite.co.uk

Performing Arts Media Rights Association

Third Floor, 161 Borough High Street, London SE1 1HR

Tel: (020) 7378 9720
Fax: (020) 7407 2008
Email: office@pamra.org.uk

PPL (Phonographic Performance Ltd)

One Upper James Street, London W1 3HG
Tel: (020) 7534 1000
Fax: (020) 7534 1111

PRS (Performing Right Society)

29-33 Berners Street, London W1P 4AA
Tel: (020) 7580 5544
Fax: (020) 7306 4050
Email: info@prs.co.uk

Student Radio Association

The Radio Academy, 5 Market Place, London W1N 7AH
Tel: (020) 7255 2010
Fax: (020) 7255 2029
Email: sra-exec@studentradio.org

press and PR companies

Absolute PR

Hazlehurst Barn, Valley Road, Derbyshire SK22 2JP
Tel: 01663 747 970
Fax: 0870 0543673

Appetite

142E Elgin Avenue, London W9 2NS
Tel: (020) 7289 9727
Fax: (020) 7289 9728
Email: appetite@easynet.co.uk

Assassination Music Promotions

Tudor House, Pinstone Way, Gerrards Cross, Buckinghamshire SL9 7BJ
Tel: 01753 893665
Fax: 01753 889888
Email: amp@assassination.co.uk

Buzz Publicity

192 Glasgow Road, Perth PH2 0NA
Tel: 01738 638140
Fax: 01738 638140
Email: dave@radiotones.com

Cutting Edge PR

Littleton House, Littleton Road, Ashford, Middlesex TW15 1UU
Tel: 01784 423214
Fax: 01784 251245

Excess Press

72-80 Leatherlane, London EC1N 7TR

Tel: (020) 7405 6226
Fax: (020) 7405 6116
Email: xspress@xspress.demon.co.uk

Get It On PR

13 Fairhazel Gardens, London NW6 3QE
Tel: (020) 7328 4916
Fax: (020) 7482 5599

Hall Or Nothing

11 Poplar Mews, Uxbridge Road, London W12 7JS
Tel: (020) 8740 6288
Fax: (020) 8749 5982
Email: press@hallornothing.com

Monkey Business PR

57D Hatton House, Hatton Garden, London EC1N 8HP
Tel: (020) 7242 3424
Fax: (020) 7242 3267
Email: monkey.pr@clara.net

Pacific Edge Promotions And Public Relations

Charlestone House, 34 Poppleton Road, London E11 1LR
Tel: (020) 8530 7748
Fax: (020) 8530 2571

The Quite Great Co

12A The White Building, High Street, Cambridge CB1 5DH
Tel: 01223 880111
Fax: 01223 882277
Email: thequitegreatcompany@btinternet.com

Slice PR

9 Apollo House, 18 All Saints Road, London W11 1HH
Tel: (020) 7221 2241
Fax: (020) 7221 1554
Email: slice@slice.co.uk

Talk Loud PR

6-10 Lexington Street, London W1R 3HS
Tel: (020) 7734 1133
Fax: (020) 7734 7787
Email: talkloud@talkloud.co.uk

Work Hard PR

19D Pinfold Road, London SW16 2SL
Tel: (020) 8677 8466
Fax: (020) 8677 5374
Email: enquiries@workhardpr.demon.co.uk

The Wright Publicity

1 Agnes Road, London W3 7RE
Tel: (020) 8749 0115
Fax: (020) 8248 3409

music publications

Billboard

23 Ridgmount Street, London WC1E 7 AH
Tel: (020) 7323 6686
Fax: (020) 7323 2314
Email: 100655.517@compuserve.com

Birmingham What's On

28 Colmore Circus, Queensway, Birmingham, West Midlands
B4 6AX
Tel: 0121 212 4141
Fax: 0121 212 2468
Email: mim.co.uk

Blues & Soul

153 Praed Street, London W2 1RL
Tel: (020) 7402 7708
Fax: (020) 7224 8227
Email: editorial@blues&soul.demon.co.uk

City Life

164 Deansgate, Manchester M60 2RD
Tel: 0161 839 1416
Fax: 0161 839 1488
Email: citylife@mcr-evening-news.co.uk

The Crack

Tel: 0191 230 3038
Crack House, 1 Pink Lane, Newcastle-Upon-Tyne NE1 5DW
Fax: 0191 230 4484
Email: gossip@crack.demon.co.uk

Fanzine

Riff Raff Productions, PO Box 1900, London N5 1EP
Tel: (020) 7226 4695
Fax: (020) 7226 4695
Email: riffraff@compuserve.com

Folk Roots

PO Box 337, London N4 1TW
Tel: (020) 8340 9651
Fax: (020) 8348 5626
Email: froots@froots.demon.co.uk

Gig UK

2nd Floor, 65 George Street, Oxford OX1 2BE
Tel: 01865 798 795
Fax: 01865 798796
Email: nbr@bandreg.com

Kerrang!

EMAP Metro, Mappin House, 4 Winsley Street, London W1R 7AR
Tel: (020) 7436 1515
Fax: (020) 7312 8910

Making Music

Nexus House, Azalea Drive, Swanley, Kent BR8 8HY
Tel: 01322 660070
Fax: 01322 616319
Email: makingmusic@cerbernet.co.uk

Melody Maker

IPC Music Magazines, Kings Reach Tower, Stamford Street, London SE1 9LS
Tel: (020) 7261 6229
Fax: (020) 7261 6706

Metal Hammer

Dennis Publishing, 19 Bolsover Street, London W1P 7HJ
Tel: (020) 7631 1433
Fax: (020) 7917 7655
Email: ed@metalhammer.demon.co.uk

Mojo

EMAP Metro, Mappin House, 4 Winsley Street, London W1R 7AR
Tel: (020) 7436 1515

Fax: (020) 7312 8296
Email: mojo@ecm.emap.com

Music Week

Miller Freeman Entertainment, 8 Montague Close, London SE1 9UR
Tel: (020) 7940 8500
Fax: (020) 7407 7094

Musician

Rhinegold Publishing, 241 Shaftsbury Avenue, London WC2H 8EH
Tel: (020) 7333 1733
Fax: (020) 7333 1736
Email: 100546.1127@compuserve.com

New Musical Express

IPC Music Magazines, Kings Reach Tower, Stamford Street, London
SE1 9LS
Tel: (020) 7261 5813
Fax: (020) 7261 5185

North Country Music

455 Alfreton Road, Nottingham, Nottinghamshire NG7 5LX
Tel: 0115 942 2615
Fax: 0115 942 2359

Paint It Red

57-59 Melbourne Street, Newcastle-Upon-Tyne, Tyne And Wear NE1 2JQ
Tel: 0191 261 1902
Fax: 0191 232 9328

Q

EMAP Metro, Mappin House, 4 Winsley Street, London W1R 7AR
Tel: (020) 7436 1515
Fax: (020) 7312 8247

Select

EMAP Metro, Mappin House, 4 Winsley Street, London W1R 7AR
Tel: (020) 7436 1515
Fax: (020) 7312 8250
Email: select@dial.pipex.com

Songlink International

23 Belsize Crescent, London NW3 5QY
Tel: (020) 7794 2540

Fax: (020) 7794 7393
Email: david@songlink.demon.co.uk

Time Out

251 Tottenham Court Road, London W1A 0AB
Tel: (020) 7813 3000
Fax: (020) 7813 6158

Top

Tower Records, 62-64 Kensington High Street, London W8 4PE
Tel: (020) 7938 5388
Fax: (020) 7937 5024
Email: mail@topmag.demon.co.uk

Uncut

IPC Music Magazines, Kings Reach Tower, Stamford Street, London
SE1 9LS
Tel: (020) 7261 6992
Fax: (020) 7261 5573

distributors

Absolute Marketing And Distribution

112 Beckenham Road, Beckenham, Kent BR3 4RH
Tel: (020) 8663 0301
Fax: (020) 8663 0302

Amato Distribution

Units 13-14, Barley Shotts Business Park, 246 Acklam Road, London W10 5YG
Tel: (020) 8964 3302
Fax: (020) 8964 3312

Backs Records

St Mary's Works, St Mary's Plain, Norwich, Norfolk NR3 3AF
Tel: 01603 624290
Fax: 01603 619999

Cargo Records (UK) Limited

17 Heathmans Road, London SW6 4TJ
Tel: (020) 7731 5125
Fax: (020) 7731 3866

Caroline 2

56 Standard Road, London NW10 6ES
Tel: (020) 8961 2919
Fax: (020) 8961 1873

CM Distribution

North Works, Hook Stone Park, Harrogate, North Yorkshire HG2 7DB
Tel: 01423 888979
Fax: 01423 885761

Direct Distribution

50 Stroud Green Road, London N4 3EF
Tel: (020) 7281 3465
Fax: (020) 7281 5671

Global Dance Distribution

The Basement, The Saga Centre, 326 Kensal Road, London W10 5BZ
Tel: (020) 8969 9333
Fax: (020) 8960 7010

Golds

Gold House, 69 Flempton Road, London E10 7NL
Tel: (020) 8539 2600
Fax: (020) 8539 2176

Kudos Records

79 Fortess Road, London NW5 1AG
Tel: (020) 7482 4555
Fax: (020) 7482 4551

Lasgo Exports

Unit 2, Chapmans Park Industrial Estate, 378-388 High Road, London
NW10 2DY
Tel: (020) 8459 8800
Fax: (020) 8451 5555

Lightning Export

Units 3-4, Northgate Business Centre, Crown Road, Enfield, Middlesex
EN1 1TG
Tel: (020) 8805 5151
Fax: (020) 8805 5252

Pinnacle

Electron House, Cray Avenue, St Mary's Cray, Orpington, Kent BR5 3RJ
Tel: 01689 870622
Fax: 01689 878269

RMG Distribution

43-51 Wembley Hill Road, Wembley, Middlesex HA9 8AU
Tel: (020) 8903 0360
Fax: (020) 8782 4706

3mv

City Network House, 81-83 Weston Street, London SE1 3RS

Tel: (020) 7378 8866
Fax: (020) 7278 8855

Vital Distribution

338a Ladbroke Grove, London W10 5AH
Tel: (020) 8324 2400
Fax: (020) 8324 0001